DISCLAIMER

This book is written specifically for those who are struggling with substance abuse, and I use terms like "drink," "smoke," "use," and others that are similar to describe the act of using substances to get intoxicated or high. I do not have any direct experience with or knowledge of other forms of addiction, including sex, gambling, food, shopping, or internet-related addictions. The tools and concepts in this book likely have application to all forms of addiction, but it is important to note the distinction and seek direct help for your specific addiction if needed.

This book is also not a resource for people needing mental health treatment or a substitution for detoxing or going to rehab. If you are dealing with opioids, heroin, or any serious substance and you have reached a level of addiction where your body is no longer in control, please seek professional assistance. Remember, even the best laid plan to overcome addiction only works if you're alive to do it.

If you are in a position where you want to consider treatment options before continuing, I've provided a brief breakdown of a few different types of initial treatment and recovery options that I believe can be beneficial, depending on your circumstances. You can find this in the glossary.

DON'T CALL ME SOBER,

CALL ME MAY

A RULE-BREAKER'S GUIDE TO
OVERCOMING ADDICTION

DON'T CALL ME SOBER CALL ME MAY

MAY TAL

HOUNDSTOOTH
PRESS

COPYRIGHT © 2025 MAY TAL
All rights reserved.

DON'T CALL ME SOBER, CALL ME MAY
A Rule-Breaker's Guide to Overcoming Addiction

FIRST EDITION

ISBN 978-1-5445-4839-5 *Hardcover*
      978-1-5445-4837-1 *Paperback*
      978-1-5445-4836-4 *Ebook*

For April and Tim.

I love you more than words and miss you every day.

CONTENTS

Introduction 13

PART I: WHY AA DOESN'T WORK

   A Broken Rule System 25
1. Addiction Isn't an Identity 27
2. Brainwashing 31
3. Forced Powerlessness 35
4. Codependency Masquerading as Community 39
5. The Never-Ending Cycle of the AA Effect 43
6. A Strange History 49
7. Married to an Outdated Approach 55
8. 12 Steps to…Nowhere 59
9. The Anonymous Way of Existing 65
10. Chronic Suppression 69
11. Tangent: Al-Anon 71
12. The Repetitive Dance 75
   Conclusion 77

PART II: OLD SELF TO NEW SELF

    Breaking the Rules 81
1. The Old Self 83
2. Calendars vs. Growth 87
3. Sponsors vs. Coaching 93
4. Meetings vs. Support 103
5. Relapsing vs. Rewiring 109
6. Coping vs. Overcoming 119
7. Denial vs. Awareness 123
8. Religious Dogma vs. Spiritual Freedom 131
9. Shame vs. Gratitude 137
10. Dependency vs. Healthy Relationships 143
11. Temptation vs. Motivation 153
12. The New Self 163

    Options for Treatment and Assistance 169
    Acknowledgments 175
    May's Recommended Readings and Teachings 177

"Believing in anonymous groups is like saying you believe bitching, moaning, and complaining accomplishes anything.

Believing in the power you have within yourself to overcome your addiction, however, says something quite different."

—MAY TAL

INTRODUCTION

THIS ISN'T ABOUT ME

What sober is to most is not what sober is to me.

To be "sober" is to be in a habitual state of not drinking. Or using. To me, the word was invented as an aspirational sort of thing. A word designed for people who want to *try* to change. But if we're being honest with ourselves—the same way I'm going to be honest with you—to *try* and to *change* are two very different things.

For me, the word "sober" contains a sense of never-ending struggle. It's a powerful but dangerous word that many use as an energetic symbol to abstain and suffer through this idea of sobriety. "Just one day at a time," the self-declared sober folks say. I don't know about you, but I think "one day at a time" sounds like a pretty shitty way to approach the rest of your life. There are problems with the way we talk about addiction nowadays. I won't sugarcoat it; the current method of joining 12-step programs, going to meetings, having sponsors, and all the rest of it is kinda, sorta...bullshit. Actually, not kinda or sorta—the bullshit becomes pretty humorous and easy to spot when you really think about it. But we'll get to that. For now, let's start at the root of the problem.

The underlying issue is this: Anonymous is forced. Made friendly by creating an atmosphere that revolves around the security blanket of your so-called God, washed down with burned coffee and passive recitation of the gospel of the beloved 12 Steps. They say, "The first step is to admit you have a problem," but that's just some surface-level BS that sounded nice for the pamphlet.

Want to know the real first step? Moving from admitting you have a problem to admitting you have created a problem.

The truth is that being sober is not an accomplishment. Overcoming your addiction, however, is.

It's easy to tell yourself that it isn't your fault. It's hereditary. It's a disease beyond your control. Blah blah blah. The lies and excuses you're telling yourself paint this neat little picture that the reason you got into drugs and alcohol is you were born or pressured into it. As if there's no way out. As if there was no other choice.

That's one of the reasons that after nineteen years of not using drugs, I don't call myself sober. I don't attend meetings, mark off days on a calendar, or collect sobriety chips. I don't believe in the kind of magical force that comes with such an idea. Instead, I believe in tapping into our natural state. I believe in our ability to take responsibility for our own lives and solve our own problems. So I bet on myself. And as a result, I ended up overcoming myself.

I believe that once you come to terms with your issues (you know, those shameful, ugly ones at the core of your addiction) and deal with them head-on, there is no more abstaining. And therefore, there is no longer an addiction.

I made some choices. I was an addict. Just like you, I caused problems for myself and others, hung out with the wrong crowd, damaged my health, and lost everything and myself along the way. I'm going to tell you a little bit about myself, but not too much. Because at the end of the day this book isn't about me.

It's about you.

MY STORY

I'll keep this short and sweet.

I had a very different upbringing than most people I know. Especially most Americans. I was born into a large Middle Eastern family and raised in Israel. We were very family-oriented and constantly surrounded by love. Our environment also included constant bomb threats, nearby explosions, and sirens blaring throughout the city.

When a long siren went off, it was to let you know that you had thirty seconds to grab your gas masks and head down to the bomb shelter. A single flat siren told you it was safe to return to your home. I was never quite sure how long we'd be down there; it's easy to lose track of time when you're praying for your life.

So yeah, just a lovely, normal childhood...right?

When I was ten, my dad got a job that moved our family to San Francisco. Like any other ten-year-old, I had no idea who I was yet. I was also very unaware of what modern science teaches us today about how the events and circumstances of our early years play a major role in shaping the people we grow up to be. There were a few things that seemed small at the time that I would later realize created the underlying roots of my addiction.

I'll tell you more about that later.

When I was a teenager, I had a best friend named April. We were April and May. Adorable, right? One day when we were fifteen, April took us to some random parking lot and pulled out a bag she'd stolen from her sister.

"What is it?" I asked.

"I think we snort it," she replied.

So we did. But I didn't feel anything. I mean, we had been smoking weed together for a while at that point, so whatever this was, it didn't seem like a big deal. The next day, we woke up and decided to do it again, but more this time. The euphoria that followed was like nothing I had ever experienced. It was the greatest feeling ever; I had never felt more alive. I still remember the thought I had after getting high on meth for the first time. I just couldn't wait to do it again. So I kept doing it. And I'll never forget the words I told April after that moment. The moment that would change the next seven years of my life. I grabbed her by the shoulders and excitedly shook her as I said, "April, we're never not doing this."

The seven-year span that followed was filled with much of what you might expect from a meth addict:

- I left my family.
- I left my friends.
- I was exploited sexually.
- I performed sexual favors for drugs.
- I sold drugs.
- I had my apartment raided by the police.
- I got picked up by the police. Twice.
- I overdosed. Twice.
- At one point, I weighed seventy-one pounds. I ended up in the hospital with excruciating chest pains only to find out that I had gotten so thin that my rib cage had started protruding from my chest.
- I had everything I owned stolen from me.
- I went on benders. Oh, the crazy stories I could tell you...
- I lost my two best friends to overdoses.
- I lost satisfaction in anything other than using. And every come-down made me want to kill myself.

I won't bore you by going deeper into the details of these events because, once again, this isn't that type of book. I'll sprinkle in a few tidbits here and there, but all you really need to know is that I went through the full spectrum of experiences with my addiction.

Then one day, I woke up. And that's when everything changed.

When I tell my story now, whether to people in my personal life or addicts I work with as a certified addiction recovery coach, it's sometimes hard for people to understand what I mean when I say that I had an awakening that completely changed the direction of my life. In modern culture, there's really no precedent for someone to go from being addicted to meth—or any drug, for that matter—to one day waking up transformed and realizing that they're done with it. That they are ready to move on. You see, we live in a culture where the first thing people think of when they think about addiction is Anonymous groups. Whether it be AA for alcoholics, NA for narcotics addiction, or any extension of the organization, most people think about 12-step programs, weekly meetings, and happy-go-lucky sponsors as the means of getting "sober." But my story, and how I overcame my addiction, is very different.

You see, shortly after my awakening, I started to develop a methodology based on principles that actually make sense for the modern world we live in. Not some faith-based bullshit developed in the 1930s. Trust me, we'll get to that too. For now, I just want you to understand that the way I overcame addiction, changed my life, became a successful founder and CEO of an IT company, and developed a coaching practice to help people who are currently struggling with addiction was through a set of actions that anyone can apply to change their own life. No "lifelong addict" bullshit. No "I have a disease I cannot overcome" excuses. None of it.

And as you might have guessed, that's what this book is about.

Unlike most "self-help" books, I'm not going to sit here and tell you that if you just apply my personal playbook to your own life, all your problems will magically go away. You can't put lipstick on a pig and expect it to win a beauty pageant. Nor can you copy and paste *my* personal discoveries to solve the issues at the core of *your* addiction. Because as convenient as that might be, it just isn't how this works.

If you were hoping to read just another inspiring addict-turned-success story, let me ask you a question: why do you feel the need to read other people's experiences in order to justify your own? My journey is unique to my own life—the good, the bad, and the really ugly parts of my past. On some level, I know that it would be easier that way. To disconnect from your own mistakes, your own shame, and your lack of ability to take responsibility for your actions. But this isn't a bedtime story. So from here on out, we're going to focus on you. The tales I've sprinkled in from my past life serve as examples of certain aspects of my methodology, but understand that this book is about giving *you* the raw materials you can use to rebuild your own life.

I don't know what events have led you here. Perhaps you've tried AA meetings or have attempted to quit on your own. You might have had friends throw you surprise interventions or your family throw you into rehab. Maybe you've lost everything. Or maybe you're just lost. Throughout this book, I'm going to give you some tough love. The same type of tough love I had to give myself along my own journey.

And if I call you out, it's probably because you need to hear it.

This book is broken down into two parts. In Part I, I'll give you twelve reasons 12-step programs don't work. I don't want to spoil the fun, but I will be picking apart every aspect of the AA way of thinking to such a violent degree that by the end, I'm confident that a certain percentage of you will have doused the book in gasoline and set it on fire.

Which is just fine by me.

For the rest of you who actually enjoy the idea of doing things a different way—like oh, I don't know...taking accountability for your own life and learning how to carve your way into a better future (one that is free from both addiction and AA meetings)—then Part II: Old Self to New Self will get you to wake the hell up, get you to smell the roses, and show you the difference between this and that.

This book is structured with the same methodology any great coach would use to help a client have a breakthrough, but specifically for addiction. It breaks down all the reasons that both 12-step programs and your current approach to recovering from addiction have not worked, are not working, and will never work for you. Because if you can't truly see where you're going wrong, you'll never overcome yourself to actually change.

So where does this argument begin?

In 12-step programs and Anonymous groups, they tell you that as an addict, you are diseased. You are powerless, and you must submit to their idea of God in order to break free from your addiction to your drug of choice. Maybe worst of all, they tell you that once you become an addict, you are an addict for life.

I choose to look at it in a different way. Today and every day, I choose the way I walk in the world with the only thing I truly have: the timestamp placed on this body that I carry with me forever. My present self is not burdened by the mistakes of my past. I don't force myself to be who I am. I just am. Every day I wake up, and I'm just *me*. It's not something I feel the need to break free from. There is only one voice that exists inside me. It's not that of my family, my friends, a sponsor, a group, or an organization. The only voice in my head is my own.

My hope is that you take what you learn in this book so that you can say the same. Sure, there will be challenges along your journey. No matter how badly you've fucked up, you can't change what you've done in the past. But you can change the person you become. After all, words have power. Some can be inspiring. Others can be limiting. Words like "sober," "recovery," and "relapse" attach an arbitrary meaning to our sense of selves and result in us carrying around unnecessary baggage for the rest of our lives. That's why, to me, there is no word to describe me and my life other than that of *being*. After all, I was brought into this world without anything. Without baggage. Without "sobriety." Without addiction.

Wholesome and pure.

No experience will ever dare call me broken.

When I was an addict, I found myself to be quite chaotic. The desire to use was uncontrollable. Or at least it felt that way. But with time, I let myself adjust to just being—and eventually I found a sense of calm in settling into my new self. I started feeling natural feelings again. I was reminded of what it was like to feel things in my body, to be at such peace. Today I gracefully and gratefully wake up a different person than I was in my past. But it's not via suppression or force. I've just naturally found a sound state of mind. I found a home in my body, and I signed the contract to own it.

My feelings, my love, my desire, my mess, my stress; it's all pure. Without that state of purity, it would mean I've been altered, tempered, or interfered with. And nothing in this world is worth giving that purity up.

So please, don't call me sober.

Call me May.

PART I

WHY AA DOESN'T WORK

A BROKEN RULE SYSTEM

I understand that the world is full of pressures to conform to the Alcoholics Anonymous way of doing things. This book is for the people who are sick and tired of it.

Specifically, those who are tired of treating addiction as an illness. Tired of looking to sponsors for salvation or validation. It's written for the addict who lives in constant struggle in their day-to-day life. The functional addict who is ready and willing to adopt a consistent routine, who wants to move forward and escape the false constructs of things like "the relapse effect," "one day at a time" mantras, and all the rest of the outdated, nonsensical advice you hear in meetings. The ones who are sick and tired of being told there is only one way to change, and it involves subscribing to a cookie-cutter approach that is designed for all but tailored to none.

AA may work for some, at least on the surface. And then there are many other people who find themselves teetering in and out of "sobriety," frustrated by the lifelong struggle that accompanies the system. This is written for the people who have tried AA or currently find themselves stuck in the revolving door of being "sober," attending meetings, going in and out of rehabs that rely on the 12 Steps, having sponsors, sponsoring others, and so on from whenever they started until the day they die. People who have tried everything and haven't found a solution. It's for those who don't want to attend meetings for the rest of their lives. Who want to face their problems head-on and carve out a new life. A better life. One that isn't spent thinking about substances or addiction but achieving the things that you currently believe to be impossible. Waking up to the truth of *you*. Living without restrictions. Finally being free. This book is for those people, written by one of their own.

I'm not rewriting the 12 Steps. I am teaching you how to move away from a helpless mindset—the one that has programmed you to think that there is nothing you can do to change the fact that you're a "lifelong addict"—and ask yourself questions that will help you retrain your mind and create a new version of yourself that is fully unshackled. Because instead of committing to the lifelong struggle, I went into the experience head-on, and I conquered it. Once you move past the AA way of thinking, you'll see that that's all addiction really is—an experience.

Some people believe there is not a single reason why someone struggling with addiction shouldn't join an Anonymous group.

I'll give you twelve.

CHAPTER 1

ADDICTION ISN'T AN IDENTITY

In AA, they like to tell you that beating your addiction requires years of constant work. It doesn't. You see, this information brainwashes millions of people to keep coming back and supporting the cause, which ultimately helps the organization grow bigger and bigger without creating long-term changes in the lives of the people participating in it.

Out of all the problems that exist within Anonymous, the core problem as it relates to you is the idea that addiction needs to be a continuous, lifelong battle that you never fully let go of. So there you are, sitting in another meeting. And another one. And another one. It's a lifelong journey, they say. So you'd better get used to having your butt ache from sitting on those cheap metal chairs!

And finally one day you look up and you realize you've been sitting in the same meetings, listening to the same stories, and regurgitating the same pithy wisdom over and over and over. Instead of surrounding yourself with people who take pleasure in cultivating a vision of a better future, you are surrounded by people addicted to the stories of their past.

You know what I mean. The excuses, the complaints. One guy woke up on the wrong side of the bed. Some girl opened up Instagram to see her ex with another woman. Let me tell you, no matter how big or small the reason, there always seems to be a convenient excuse to hurry up and suck down a gin and tonic. Or at least that seems to be the general consensus in these meetings.

Isn't it funny to think about how there's never a newcomer who walks through the door and asks, "How long is this 'recovery' going to take?" or "Wait a second...if this system works, what are all of you still doing here?" I remember asking this question in one of the first meetings I went to. Yeah, that's right: the girl writing the anti-Anonymous book spent a few months attending meetings and getting a front-row seat to their one and only exhibit: *Bitching and Moaning*, starring a bunch of people who, if we're being honest, are addicted to one thing or another to cover up the simple fact that they just don't like themselves. When I asked the question, a bitter woman turned to me and told me, "Oh dear, you will *always* be an addict." This was the very first sliver of brainwashing I received that I would later regret. But how could I blame her? It's pretty hard to have a vision of the future when you're stuck in the past.

The problem with this mindset is that it gives you an excuse to let yourself off the hook when you are tempted to slip up. So you end up just saying, "Fuck it." And just like that, they'll hand you a chip and free rein to the donuts good ole Patty brought to the meeting, which is their way of welcoming you back into their accountability-free circle of mediocrity. A common phrase used in AA is "Keep coming back—it works if you work it!" which sounds great, in theory. But it's clearly not working.

While I'm on the topic, allow me to step through the bullshit and tell you what's really going on here. These excuses aren't just rationalizing your bad behavior. They are actually manifesting these outcomes. Think about it: deep down you want to drink, so whether consciously or not, you sit around looking for negative things in your life that you can use to justify your bad behavior.

But this isn't AA, and I'm not your sponsor, so I'm going to be frank: you are the way you are because of your own actions. End of story. You don't have a disease, and your excuses are not valid. Even if your doctor found that you have an addictive-behavior disease or a predisposition to becoming an alcoholic, that's still not an excuse for the choices you make.

Look, we live in a modern world (which is exactly why I'm writing this book and not a 12-step program), and as proven by experts like Dr. Joe Dispenza and Dr. Bruce Lipton, along with Mindvalley programs and even plant medicine, there is scientific evidence that we can literally regulate our own genes. Epigenetics (influencing gene expression without altering DNA) and neuroplasticity (the brain's ability to reorganize itself by forming new neural connections) are scientifically proven to influence our ability to change the way our minds work.

Knowing this, we can use it to help restructure our minds and heal ourselves by consuming the right information from the right mentors. But if you want to continue to sit around blaming your circumstances or your disease, fine. Keep bitching and moaning for as long as you want. Be my guest.

Anonymous and 12-step programs enable these excuses and foster an environment full of addicts who will struggle toward sobriety for the rest of their lives. This book is about looking you dead in the eye and calling you out on your shit. Because once you've accepted the reality that your choices alone have led you here, that's when you can actually start to change.

CHAPTER 2

BRAINWASHING

When you hear the term *addiction*, the first thing that enters your mind is the Anonymous group.

As if there is no other option.

Here's what I don't get: You're telling me that you don't know how to live your life in a respectable way without running to a group every week to give a play-by-play of your struggle to resist the almighty temptation? That you need a pat on the back and the applause of a bunch of strangers to validate your own instincts? What are you, nine? The truth is that successful people don't need applause. And if you want to be successful in overcoming your addiction, you have to embody the behaviors of someone who is already successful. The problem is that this type of "Anonymous" mentality belittles people to such a degree that they think they're not worth anything if they aren't receiving constant validation for their "good behavior." This is where the brainwashing begins.

You have been programmed to live your life thinking and feeling that you are protected through this system. If you ever have a sudden craving, you can just run to your local meeting, and you will be saved. Over time, your actions have reinforced this kind of thinking, which makes the program harder to break free from. Your mind starts to convince you that you really are protected from your demons by this "nice" group of people. But in reality, you're just running further and further away from the problem. Burying the problem deeper and deeper within your psyche. So when you get up and say, "I *almost* relapsed today because of my disease," you are running to a meeting to...tell a story? About an event that has already passed?

Let me ask you this: are you there to tell a story of victory or to manifest more of these so-called hardships? Be honest with yourself. Are you holding on to some negative story merely for the little dopamine hits you get from recreating the drama over and over? Are you benefitting in any way from the experience, or do you just want something to continue sharing so that you can relate to the program and your fellow attendees?

People are far more impressionable than they realize, myself included. I'm not as naive these days because I've learned over time to not believe everything I hear. But when it comes to something we know nothing about, that can put us in a very vulnerable position. The reason we are all susceptible to being brainwashed is we don't investigate ourselves deeply when we're faced with something we don't have the answer to. We are suffocated by so much chatter nowadays that we can't even hear our own intuition. We're so quick to think that someone out there has the answer that we're immediately convinced by the first thing we hear.

Imagine one morning you open up social media and see an influx of not just influencers but also unqualified people who think they have it all figured out and feel the need to project their "wisdom" onto everyone. Your best friend was cheated on by her boyfriend, and now she thinks she's qualified to give a crash course on narcissism. And then an uncertified life coach thinks he's cracked the code on how to create a seven-figure business—even though he hasn't ever made seven figures himself. So there you are questioning whether the person you're currently dating is a narcissist or if you should call your boss and quit your 9-to-5 because you've unlocked the secret to getting rich quick.

Or maybe I go to the grocery store because my personal trainer is telling me to eat more protein. So I buy a shit ton of meat. But then on the way home, Spotify automatically cues up a hot new podcast about animal cruelty and factory farming and how *meat is murder*, and by the end of the podcast there I am, at home throwing $300 worth of groceries straight in the trash.

Or let's say someone walks into a car dealership. It's their first time buying a car. They get lit up hearing about all the bells and whistles—how it'll look, how they'll feel. The salesman does something more than just sell them a car; they sell them the idea that no other car could possibly be better. They get so convinced that right then and there, they don't even think to go look at another car or go to another dealership.

I'll bring this full circle: brainwashing is all around us, from inside AA meetings to the very fabric of modern life. If we aren't vigilant about the beliefs we choose to accept, someone else—whether a friend, sponsor, or salesman—will be more than happy to impose their beliefs onto us.

You see, I refuse to let any bogus information crowd my mind. My mind, my body—this is my home. Why would I ever want to place garbage in my own home, like some kid who thinks it would be funny to TP his own house? Because at the end of the day, I will be held accountable for whatever I bring into my life, and in the same way, I will be responsible for cleaning it up.

The same is true for you.

CHAPTER 3

FORCED POWERLESSNESS

When you are an addict and you want to stop being one, you have a few options. One option is to work the steps, where you will spend the remainder of your life in a constant state of suppression. Or as I would call it, agony. Another option is to deal with the underlying issues and acquire a new frame of mind—one that is different from the one that has led you to the point you're at now, which is sitting here reading a book about addiction.

When you ask a person, "Why can't you quit?" most of the time they'll beat around some bush, feeding you a sob story with a bunch of fancy words that all amount to the same thing: elaborate yet irrelevant excuses. And instead of doing the work to overcome it, they prefer to blame their problems on a disease, a genetic condition, or an event from their past.

Sound familiar?

Or perhaps you do know the answer and you just aren't ready to admit it. Because in your mind, that would be too embarrassing. Yet you're open and willing to admit that you're an addict to a bunch of strangers. How ironic that you think between addiction and embarrassment, the lesser of two evils is being an addict.

Sure, you can keep refusing to take responsibility for any of your mistakes. Go ahead and blame it on a disease or your father's genetics. Are you listening to yourself? You can't inherit this shit. What you can inherit, apparently, is whatever 100 percent organic grass-fed bullshit you hear from the people around you. Instead, take ownership of your life. Because if you don't, one day you will look back and realize that this beautiful thing called life has passed you by, and all you have to show for it is a handful of fragmented memories and desecrated relationships powered not by your addiction but by your unwillingness to overcome it.

The things that led you to being an addict are probably very human. Repressed trauma. Stress. Bad home life. Failed marriage. Self-hatred. Fear of death. Sheesh, even fear of living. The list goes on. There's nothing embarrassing about going through hard times or dealing with things that are difficult. That's just life—and sorry to tell you, but that's just the world we live in. Quit complaining, and deal with it. No, what's embarrassing is to blame your failures on external events and other people. To refuse to take responsibility for them and to wash them down with your drug of choice. That's what's embarrassing!

"My parents were addicts." Wah.

"All my friends were doing it." Wah wah.

"I needed it to cope with stress or my repressed trauma." Wah wah wah!

Let me go ahead and summarize your reasoning: nothing is your fault. You can't make your own decisions or stand up for yourself. You have no control over anything. And you're totally and helplessly powerless to the point that you are content with being a hopeless nag for the rest of your life. And then you go to the meetings to validate all of it, huh? Boy oh boy, misery sure does love company.

If you follow this line of reasoning to its natural conclusion, it will probably go something like this:

"I sure would love to change. But honestly, where can I even go from here? The meetings don't work. I'm fucked up, and my life is fucked up because there's no way out...so I guess there's no hope for me...so I might as well keep going."

Don't get me wrong. There are support groups all around the world that agree with that type of thinking. But the effect of this does the opposite of empowering you—it conditions you to become permanently powerless. As we all know, there are plenty of people who like to be coddled and told that everything they're doing is perfectly fine. They want someone to listen and nod along to every excuse they have in the tank. Well answer me this: do you really want me to coddle you? Is that why you bought this book about overcoming addiction—so that someone could gently tell you that everything is going to be all right? Because if that's the case, aren't you doing a pretty good job of coddling yourself all on your own? When you approach this process with that type of mindset, you're only trying to make yourself feel better, so you ultimately won't get anywhere—you'll only diffuse the current situational state you're in. That's what I like to call *the trouble state*. When you're in that frame of mind, you're not actually progressing toward breaking down any barriers between your addiction and your current thoughts. Coddling you won't create a change; it'll only temporarily stop a trigger until the thoughts come back around at a later time.

Welcome to adulthood! You know, the part of life where your parents aren't there to tell you, "Don't put your hand on the burner," so you have to learn the valuable lesson that if you want to stop getting burned, quit putting your fucking hand over the flames.

There are plenty of excuses to continue being an addict. Deep down, you and I both know they're all bullshit. Every single one. And yes, you can make the choice to continue living this way. You can live out the rest of your existence making excuses and refusing to face up to your problems. You can choose to remain powerless. If that's what you really want, you might as well put this book back on the shelf and get back to wasting more of your time.

But if by chance you are tired of being this weak person suckling on the sympathy of anyone who is willing to feel sorry for you, buckle up—this ride is all about unapologetic self-awareness and accountability.

CHAPTER 4

CODEPENDENCY MASQUERADING AS COMMUNITY

Before we go any further, there's something important that I need to address. Some people who read this book will be inspired to open their minds and apply these concepts to go out and create a better life. Others will be very, very unhappy with the way I talk about AA. So let me get this out of the way.

If you think that wasting away at meetings is the only answer to addiction, fine. If you're pissed at me for saying that AA isn't actually changing your life and you think that you're "clean and sober" now thanks to the program, great. This book obviously isn't for you. May the force be with you! But understand this: if your blood is boiling right now as you read these words, you are no different from a furious Christian reading a book written by an atheist or a quivering Democrat at a Republican rally. You've been conditioned by an organization to defend its honor without even considering the possibility of taking a different viewpoint. To continue blindly upholding its values and professing its blessings.

You don't have to take it personally. After all, it's not your fault that AA is chock-full of illogical, irrational issues. You'll just have to excuse me as I go ahead and poke a few more holes.

First, let's break down what you like about going to meetings. You like the fact that you get to be surrounded by others who are suffering too. You sit there day in and day out, sharing stories of addiction, listening to stories about addiction, and thinking about stories of addiction. It makes you feel less shitty knowing that there are a bunch of other people out there struggling just like you. You like the communal nature of working together to resist that great temptation to drink. One more hour of sobriety! Day 7! Month 8!

Excuse me for saying that devoting yourself to a lifetime of meetings is a pathetic way to live. The reason I say this is I've been there, and I fucking promise you there is more to life. Also, wake up, girlfriend! Tomorrow is not guaranteed. That's not a cliché. It's the cold, hard truth.

Speaking of something else cold and hard, as I said before, I've spent plenty of time myself sitting on those metal folding chairs arranged in the perfect shape for a good old-fashioned circle jerk of self-loathing. I know this might be hard to hear, but I realized that if I'm seeking out friends for relatability who are constantly struggling with their own demons, we're only going to be dragging each other down. I'm not saying that addicts should avoid each other. But if neither person knows how to build the other up, you have a perfect recipe for trouble.

The truth is that you need to surround yourself with people who take responsibility for themselves. People who thrive not only on accomplishing their goals but on pushing forward with the understanding that there is always more to gain and further to grow. And when they make mistakes, they are quick to admit their own faults and tune in to their own strengths, skills, and instincts to continue working on themselves and giving their best to everything they do.

It's great to learn from others. It's great to have a mentor you can go to when you need advice. But the difference between a mentor and a sponsor—the key difference—is that a mentor is not someone you call on every day to complain about your life and rely on to keep you from spiraling back into using. A mentor is like the father who teaches his teenage son how to shave. A sponsor is like one who never stops changing his son's diapers.

Chances are, you are a grown-ass person. Start acting like one.

Personally, I run away from people who exist in a constant state of living in the past. In my few short months in AA, I was forced to swallow so much bullshit that now I can smell it a mile away. I hope this doesn't hurt your feelings, but here's one of my truths when it comes to growth: I refuse to go down with the ship. I would rather jump off and swim to shore alone than be stuck on that boat with people who will weigh me down to the point where I eventually drown too.

This goes both ways. If you don't want to help yourself, you can't start latching onto people and forcing others to go down in flames with you. Why do you think the expression "puff puff pass" exists? Why do you think meth addicts and stoners are so eager to pass around the pipe? And why are alcoholics always trying to coerce their buddies into having a drink by repeating the phrase, "Hey, man, don't make me drink alone"? We all know why. Getting other people to join in on the so-called "fun" makes you feel less alone. It also makes you feel like you're not crazy for doing what you do. But whether you're the friend trying to stay clean or the one passing around the blunt, deep down you know that those kinds of friendships aren't going to work out.

Not if anyone involved is serious about making a change, at least.

Lastly, have you ever noticed that going to meetings is a lot like sitting in a confessional?

"Where do I start, Father?"

"It's simple, son. You confess your sins, and through me, the Lord will forgive you."

"That's it?"

They make it all sound so easy. If you ever screw up again, it's all good! Just come on back, and we'll welcome you with open arms! Zero down; twelve steps to go!

You see? Just like walking in and out of a confessional.

CHAPTER 5

THE NEVER-ENDING CYCLE OF THE AA EFFECT

Ladies and gentlemen, please tell me this: if AA really does work, why are people who have been "clean and sober" for ten years still attending meetings? Instead of making any sort of real change, they substitute the time they wasted getting high for... wasting time bitching and moaning about it? Allowing themselves to participate in this cycle means continuing living a life of the past, which is the exact life they wanted to move away from. Call me crazy, but if that is the end result of joining a 12-step program, you might as well just get high.

You must think I'm crazy for saying that. Hell, you might disagree so strongly that right now, at this very moment, you are thinking about putting this book down and coming up with a story to tell your AA group about this awful, offensive book you were reading. But stay with me for just another moment. Let's say you believe that AA has changed many people's lives for the better. Is switching one lousy life for another your definition of positive change? A life spent rehashing your past mistakes is one of regret, disappointment, and paralyzing shame. Is that really so different from being an addict?

If you have any interest in breaking free from this cycle, it's important to understand how the program is run. As I've been saying, AA is designed to brainwash people into a system that is actively corroding their ability to move past the label of being an "addict."

I should know.

You might be wondering how someone like me would end up in meetings. Was I trying to be a good girl and go the 12-step route like everyone else? Nope. I actually wasn't there to get help for my "recovery" journey—I had already figured that out on my own. The story of how I ended up in a meeting is pretty amusing in my opinion. One night, I was at a pool hall, and I met a guy named Viktor. He was super cool, so after we played I asked him if he'd like to hang out sometime. He told me that, unfortunately, he couldn't because he had a disease.

Oh no, I thought. This guy must be dying.

As he was packing up his pool cue, I lightly inquired, "May I ask what disease you have?"

"Addiction," he replied.

Funny, right? You see, Viktor (who was a very sweet guy) had been going to NA meetings for his meth addiction (and his constant "relapses"), and he said that he didn't make friends with people who weren't in the program. You should have seen the look on his face when I told him that I used to be addicted to meth too. *Phew, looks like we could be friends after all!*

Viktor invited me to a meeting, which confused me at first. Didn't you say you *used* to be an addict? *Same here, man. Why are you still attending?* Sure enough, he began preaching the gospel of NA and convinced me to join him. And trust me, even back then I told him I didn't need any help with my addiction. I told him that I was done with it. He said, "Well, why don't you come anyway? Maybe you'll make some friends."

Looking back, it's funny to think how that decision, and the few months I spent going to Anonymous groups, ended up being the thing that led me to "relapse."

More on that in Part II.

I mean, it does sound nice in theory. A group of self-proclaimed warriors fighting the good fight against the war of substance abuse. The promise of structure, support, and very convincing testimonials from an army of people who are quick to praise the magic of the institution. But when I took a step back and started to think about it logically, the entire system began to fall apart.

Placing restrictions on sexual relationships—who are these people, high school sex hall monitors? Like, who do you have to bribe to get a free pass? Taking care of a plant for a year before you can go on a date? Will your sponsor be stopping by from time to time to check if the plant is still alive? Who came up with this stuff?

Oh, that's right: to be a good little AA member, you have to suppress all your core human emotions to be allowed into the next phase of your life. When you start to really look at it, AA begins to feel a lot less like a support group for addicts and more like a cult for fanatics who need to latch on to something in order to justify their own actions. Not to mention control others with their silly little mantras and rituals. Looking back at my own experience in meetings, I'm honestly a little surprised that they don't charge a fee at the door or present members with a leader to worship.

When I think back on Viktor, it actually made a lot of sense why he was so committed to the meetings. I realized that for people who were stuck in the cycle of "being sober"—"relapsing"—"being sober"—"relapsing," meetings felt like the perfect place to go and try to straighten themselves out. It's a program that allows people to white-knuckle it until the clock runs out and they "relapse" and eventually end up right back at square one.

"But you don't understand, May. My sister is now sober because of AA." Oh yeah? And what is she doing now? Wasting countless hours driving to the nearest AA meeting so she can tell herself she's imprisoned by her own "forever-addict mind."

The problems with AA go beyond the organization itself. At the end of the day, that's for them and their devoted followers to worry about. The bigger question, as it relates to you, is this: why should you keep yourself in a state of constant suffering? Sitting in meetings every week is just about as good as punching a time clock for a paycheck that's never going to get cut. The actual solution requires self-awareness, self-teaching, and self-discipline. It's about doing your own self-work to uncover and accept the realities of your past experiences and create a future where you start living your life on your own terms. Where you, your actions, and your well-being are not dependent on anything outside of yourself.

If this concept sounds strange, let me give you an example. Picture a turtle. Every day the turtle wakes up and wanders from place to place. But no matter where he goes, he's always home because by his very nature he can't run away from himself. The same thing is true for you and me. As the saying goes, wherever you go, there you are. Like the turtle, you can't run away from yourself either. Despite what your parents, friends, and sponsors might tell you, when you run away from your problems, you end up running right back to your addiction. So by facing yourself and your problems, you have the potential to create a new path for your life—one that goes forward instead of backward. This can be scary, but it's also freeing. You don't need a meeting, a group, or a sponsor to get you through the hard times. For better or worse, it's up to you.

Part of this mindset shift comes in understanding just how much nonsense exists in the Anonymous way of thinking. For example, let's talk about the name itself. Alcoholics Anonymous. Why is it anonymous? Are you actually ashamed of your name? Are you really so ashamed of yourself and your addiction that you have to hide in a dark room surrounded by other shadows just to keep you company? And if you are, how come you've never questioned yourself as to why?

Just because you've made mistakes *does not* mean you have to carry the shame and guilt with you. Trust me. In my addict days I did plenty of things that most people would feel deeply shameful about.

> ### FRAGMENT—2001-ISH
>
> It's 2:17 a.m. I haven't slept in...god knows how long. I'm guessing this is day six of the bender.
>
> I desperately need sleep. Not because I'm tired but because I know that getting some rest is the only way I can fully feel the high again.
>
> I walk into the living room and ask my friend to put me to sleep. He follows me to my bedroom. This isn't anything new for us. As he begins to ball up his fist, I catch a glimpse of myself in the mirror. Huh. Looks like I do this so often that my eyes don't even bruise anymore. How funny.
>
> I turn to look back at my friend as the chafed, sharp bones of his right knuckles are just about to make contact with my left eye.
>
> I wake up twenty-four hours later.

AA is well-known for creating and spreading the philosophy of "sobriety" and the idea of the lifelong struggle that all addicts must face. You could say I'm sort of the poster child for the opposite way of thinking. I've actually been known to give people the "don't you dare call me sober" look when they use that term. It's the look of someone who refuses to be put in that silly little box of what everyone else thinks "sober" is. I don't mean to sound like an egomaniac or too prideful, but I'm nothing like those people.

I had my experiences, and now they're in my past. I've learned from them. I've gained knowledge and insight into myself and the human condition that most people will never admit to. But by facing them directly, I've been able to take what is useful and leave the rest behind—without the help of any Anonymous group.

Don't you think it's time for you to move on too?

CHAPTER 6

A STRANGE HISTORY

There's a lot about AA that most people don't know. It seems like no matter who you ask, you'll hear a different story about how Anonymous groups came to be. After all, isn't everything just a version of what *really* happened? Don't quote me, but some of the stories, as I understand them, go a little something like this:

AA was created by a man named Bill Wilson, who AA-goers refer to as Bill W. The idea for the 12 Steps came after Bill W's doctor told him that alcoholism is an illness and an allergy and that apparently Bill had this allergy real bad. I must say, bravo, mystery doctor from the 1930s. Bra-a-a-vo! You've cracked the code. I speak for all of us when I say I'm glad your highly intelligent medical diagnosis laid the framework for an addiction recovery program still widely used today. I mean, apparently everyone is having an allergic reaction nowadays.

After receiving his diagnosis, Bill W went to a rehab facility to try to alleviate his "symptoms." And that's where it hit him. At that moment, Bill W claimed to see the light. Yes, that light.

The bright white light that many addicts have since claimed to see after being taught about the experiences of their beloved founder.

Pretty convenient, huh?

Along his journey, Bill W had developed what I call a "tick" to "relapse," and Bill's doctor suggested he seek out another alcoholic to discuss it with. He then met a doctor named Bob Smith who was so inspired by Bill's story that he soon decided to move Bill and Bill's wife into their family home to help them spread their message further. From there, Bill and Bob began conspiring an all-out crusade to save alcoholics from around the world.

The problem with good ole Bill and Bob, as it turned out, was that although they seemed to have good intentions, their execution was, well...you'll see.

Their pitch went something like this:

"We should take a bunch of people struggling with substance addiction, put them in the same room on a weekly basis, give them twelve basic steps for how to cope with this 'allergy' and see what happens."

And the idea for AA was born.

Okay, fine. That's not a direct quote, but you get the gist. From there, things somehow became even more interesting. They started bringing addicts in to stay at the Smith household, which went about as well as you might imagine. Dr. Smith's wife held Bible teachings for the addicts, which fastened the connection between Christianity and Anonymous groups that still exists today.

This brings up something interesting. If Dr. Smith and his wife had been Muslim, is it not fair to reason that AA would promote the principles of Islam? Or if they had been agnostic, would 12-step programs be less focused on the idea of "higher powers"? This is an important point because it shows the fact that all the "God" stuff in the 12 Steps is actually quite arbitrary and dependent on the religious beliefs of the people who founded the program. This is just one of many, many reasons why Anonymous groups and 12-step programs need to be questioned. And not just questioned by the masses—that's not the focus here. These programs, these rules need to be questioned by *you*.

So returning to Bill and Bob, what exactly were they trying to promote? Spirituality or religion? When you look into it, it becomes clear that the modern 12 Steps have strayed very far from the original intention of the program. Nowadays, you see people walking around treating the 12 Steps like it's their bible. But, honey, isn't the appeal of the Bible that it is supposed to be the word of God? We know for a fact that the 12 Steps were written by these two drunken fools. And do you want to know the funniest part of the whole thing? Bill and Bob didn't have it figured out for themselves. These two men decided to hit the road, ready to preach the gospel of sobriety…while they were still struggling with alcoholism. As a result, now people all around the world are "struggling with addiction forever." Sounds familiar, doesn't it? I'm not saying these men were evil or that they had bad intentions with what they were doing. I'm saying their solution just doesn't make sense. If this is a solution, why are you forever in recovery? Shouldn't you be recovered? And therefore, like I said before, wouldn't this just be a temporary experience and not a lifelong death sentence?

I'm just trying to shine a light on the fact that Bill W and Dr. Smith went off to preach the message that alcoholics are diseased and that conforming to a program and deeming yourself powerless to God are the only things keeping you from going off the rails. In today's world, we know better than that.

For the record, I don't care what your religious or spiritual beliefs are, nor should you care about mine. Regardless of what you believe, I think you would agree that each and every one of us has the power to make decisions for ourselves and hold ourselves accountable for the results. With modern science, we have the understanding that we create programs in our minds, which gives us the ability to change our life trajectories in ways that most people living in the 1930s never could have imagined.

It seems obvious when you think about it now, but why would people base their approach to addiction recovery around a strategy created by two alcoholic dudes from the thirties who didn't even have their own shit figured out? Our friend Bill was met with resistance from the organization in his later years for experimenting with LSD. Bet you didn't know about that part either, huh? So tell me this: if you're Bill W and you've figured out the one-size-fits-all solution to addiction recovery...why would you need to experiment with another drug? And instead of preaching the 12 Steps, shouldn't you change your teachings to the mystical powers of LSD?

And what about some of the less flattering details that our crusading heroes seemed to have conveniently left out of the Big

Book? Like how Bill's wife was attacked by the addicts who were living in the Smith home during their experiments, or how none of the addicts in the house were able to actually get "sober"? Not to mention that the only thing Bill wanted in the final moments of his life was for someone to bring him a glass of whiskey.

When you take a step back and look at the origins of AA, it becomes clear that the underlying foundation of the program is as shaky as the men who created it. And like a contagious virus that is difficult to contain, Bill and Bob's methodology reached pandemic-level success by spreading across the world at a rapid pace.

CHAPTER 7

MARRIED TO AN OUTDATED APPROACH

This may be obvious to some, but let's stop for a moment and talk a little more about how outdated these ideas are. Back in 1938, when the 12 Steps were written, most people worked manual labor jobs and the country was still recovering from the Great Depression. Cars weren't all that common yet, most Americans didn't have a television, and women couldn't even get a loan without a man cosigning for them. So *why the fuck* would we base our entire approach to addiction recovery around a method that has simply not evolved with the times? We have had so many breakthroughs in science and technology that inform the way we think about addiction. And not only do we have access to so much more than people living in the 1930s, but we ourselves are the key to our ability to access so much more. We have moved past the point where it makes any sense to brand ourselves with the "always an addict" stamp we place on our foreheads.

Ugh. Excuse me while I gag at the thought of this...

Okay, I'm back. I mean, just think about it! Back then, people lived in a state of fear. In modern times, we have the opportunity to live in a state of abundance. In 1938, the concept of "finding God" meant a whole lot more than it does now. Nowadays, most people have been exposed to so many new things that we all have the freedom to explore the big questions for ourselves instead of listening to some authority figure who calls their disciples into weekly meetings to preach the gospel of "the Holy 12 Steps."

This is not to say that there wasn't merit to what Bill W and the original AA folks tried to do. At that point in time, the thing they created (even if very flawed) might have been better than nothing. But that doesn't change the fact that none of the 12 Steps truly break down the fundamental subjects that are present in today's society. They don't address the things we actually struggle with today.

Also, riddle me this: why does AA have a 5–10 percent "success rate"? What exactly equates to success? Abstinence? It's laughable to think that this worldwide phenomenon is the go-to for people struggling with addiction. It's like the world has given up. Don't get me wrong. I'm not dismissing the experience of those of you who are struggling with addiction and have tried AA as a solution. I'm just dismissing the silly little idea that these 100-year-old twelve steps of generic bullshit are the best solution for anyone going through the very real challenge of addiction. Just in case I wasn't clear before.

I'm on a mission to pioneer the next wave of people to overcome their addiction—rather than just coping with it. Because in truth, I can't change what AA does. But for people who are looking for another way, I can take responsibility for helping you pave your own path. I mean, hell, someone's gotta do it. Specifically, someone who cares enough about people like you that they are willing to take all the hate and pushback that will inevitably come from writing this book and going up against such a large and powerful organization. So for better or worse, I'm charging forward with a smile on my face and zero fucks to give about what anyone else has to say about it.

CHAPTER 8

12 STEPS TO... NOWHERE

Let me tell you what comes to my mind when I read the 12 Steps.

Step 1: We admitted we were powerless over alcohol—that our lives had become unmanageable.

We? No, *you* admit that you're an idiot, accept the fact that you "using" isn't a collective choice, and stop making the excuse that you have no power over yourself. If you can use your hands to pick up a drink and your mouth to smoke from a pipe, I'm pretty sure you have the power to choose everything you do and don't do. You're not incompetent...or are you? If so, it's probably best if you go hit that meeting.

Step 2: We came to believe that a Power greater than ourselves could restore us to sanity.

Ummm...isn't your higher power supposed to be *you*? Oh, is

this your invisible friend who's greater and more powerful than you? Dope, bro. How much does he bench?

Step 3: We made a decision to turn our will and our lives over to the care of God as we understood Him.

Wait a second. God is a "He"? Sorry, I didn't realize we were still living in the 1930s. Some women are about to be so pissed.

Step 4: We made a searching and fearless moral inventory of ourselves.

For crying out loud! So what, now you have to rehash everything that happened? When are you ever supposed to focus on anything new or on "recovering" if all your energy is being spent on the old "fucked-up" you?

Step 5: We admitted to God, to ourselves, and to another human being the exact nature of our wrongs.

So now you have to dump all your disgusting past onto someone else to confirm that it's true? Ahem, I'm pretty sure you were there to witness it yourself. Remember all those regrettable things you did? That should be enough of a confirmation, man. Move the fuck on!

Step 6: We were entirely ready to have God remove all these defects of character.

Boy oh boy. Where can I get one of these magic pills? And can we take this every time we do something wrong? How about you start removing your own defects of...no, sorry, you're right. I sound crazy.

Step 7: We humbly asked Him to remove our shortcomings.

You'd better keep this thing hidden because I'm about to fight you for this genie lamp.

Step 8: We made a list of all persons we had harmed, and became willing to make amends to them all.

Oh great, more shame! Haven't you gotten the memo? The only way to do right by your loved ones is to better yourself. You've apologized. Great! From there it becomes the other person's job to recognize that your toxicity wasn't about them in the first place.

Step 9: We made direct amends to such people wherever possible, except when to do so would injure them or others.

Wait. Now I need to repeat Steps 4 and 5 again? Aw man, the nightmare continues. I thought I was almost to the end!

Step 10: We continued to take personal inventory and when we were wrong promptly admitted it.

Oh my god (not literally), it doesn't stop does it? *More* bitching and whining? Geez, no wonder this drives you to drink. I'm starting to understand that 5–10 percent more and more.

Step 11: We sought through prayer and meditation to improve our conscious contact with God as we understood Him, praying only for knowledge of His will for us and the power to carry that out.

I personally believe in prayer and meditation, but "God" means something different for us all. Here's a news flash, folks: your religious beliefs don't have anything to do with your addiction. You do not have to believe in anything outside of yourself in order to change. That's a personal choice! The only thing to believe in is you, *you fool*.

Step 12: Having had a spiritual awakening as the result of these Steps, we tried to carry this message to alcoholics, and to practice these principles in all our affairs.

Whoa, whoa, whoa. If this is true, the first eleven steps worked, and you've finally had your big spiritual awakening, now you're supposed to hold the entire world accountable to fixing themselves too? Man, when do you ever get to have a life—and actually live it? You're not responsible for anyone else or anything except for living your best life. You don't have control over what other people choose to do or how they live their lives.

Geez Louise.

Basically, as I've said from the beginning, believing in the Anonymous group is like saying I believe bitching, moaning, and complaining accomplishes anything. By the time you finish reading this book, I hope that, after deciding with all your conviction to let go of the old you, you give it away to someone who needs it and move on with your own life. Unlike the 12-step programs that basically ask you to walk around with a skin-colored tattoo on your forehead that says *addict*, I want you to take the lessons you learn, apply them to your own life, and go enjoy your new self.

Oh, and if you were wondering why the forehead tattoo is the same color as your skin, it's so you can continue hiding your problems away in meetings where your issues are as nameless as you are. "Hello, Mr. Anonymous," says the bartender, a.k.a. your drug dealer.

In AA, they tell you to become aware of your problem, admit it to the world, and then marry it. Marry the excuses, the complaints, the ongoing struggle.

"Of course it's not my fault!"

"I am diseased!"

"Life is hard!"

Marry it and carry it around with you for the rest of your life, never going deeper or even thinking to search for the root cause.

For the sake of argument, have you ever stopped to question why there are twelve steps for everyone, no matter who they are or what sort of addiction they're dealing with? Is twelve the magic number, meaning there is no way that three steps might be right for one person and twenty-five for another? Of course not. Because 12-step programs aren't tailored to fit the specific needs of an individual person. It's a cookie-cutter approach to a personal problem.

Even though they broke the steps down into twelve, it's really just one giant step in a spiral staircase that begins where it ends and ends where it begins. That's the problem with the Anonymous group—you sit. You talk. You complain. You're ashamed. You're validated. You're happy. Then you're sad again. The days change, and so do the excuses, but the meetings stay the same. Because you never get below the surface. You never get into the parts of your struggle that are more deeply rooted. This is why, despite going to meetings and following their precious 12 Steps, you continue going back to the substances that took you there in the first place.

CHAPTER 9

THE ANONYMOUS WAY OF EXISTING

For now, let's focus on you. As I said in the Introduction and will continue to say throughout the book, there is no quick fix that works for everyone. It varies, which means that in reality, "It just takes twelve steps" doesn't actually exist. Because they don't apply to everyone.

Bill W had his own personal awakening that led him to come up with what he felt were the twelve steps to "recovery" and then decided that his twelve steps would work for everyone else too. The questions you should be asking yourself are "Where is my *own awakening*—and what are my steps?" It's kind of absurd when you think about it. So you're telling me that everyone should follow the steps in the same order? If we are taking the 12 Steps at face value, there are steps that some people won't need to worry about and others that they may need to readdress over and over until they truly resolve the issue. We all have our own strengths and weaknesses that need to be addressed in a personal way.

You: Your day was shit. Your week has been shit. Everything's gone wrong. You decided to say, "Fuck it!" You got as high as a kite snorting rails to forget all about it and told yourself, "Oh, it's not so bad."

Anonymous solution: "Keep coming back. It works if you work it!"

You: Stopped by a buddy's house, and everyone was smoking weed, so you got high and lost four months of "sobriety."

Anonymous solution: "Keep coming back. It works if you work it!"

You: Came home after work, got in a fight with your spouse, and decided to hell with it! You went to the bar and got wasted.

Anonymous solution: "Keep coming back. It works if you work it!"

A tale as old as time.

Is this a program designed to help people or a Magic 8 Ball? Why on earth would people think that these repetitive, nonsense slogans would be the solution to their problems? How could anyone get caught up in this stuff? The reason is simple. I've said it before, and I'll say it again: AA brainwashes you. It's not just a program in the physical sense; it's *actually programming you*. You're putting your mind into the wrong kind of program that celebrates excuses and complaints and demonizes solutions that actually work.

If you ask me, we need an entirely new program because quite frankly, this one sucks.

CHAPTER 10

CHRONIC SUPPRESSION

When you're sitting there spending all this time with people who talk about how all they want to do is drink or all they want to do is smoke, you are actively placing yourself in an environment where suppressing addiction has become the standard way of life. It's just you and a bunch of people who are all digging their fingernails into their thighs and repressing every urge in their bodies to go on yet another bender.

If you have ever found yourself saying these things, then you need to understand that what you're *actually* saying is that you can't cope with life. That you don't want to deal with yourself or any of your underlying issues. That you are content to continue living a life you aren't proud of. As a result, you find yourself "relapsing" into using alcohol or drugs and then returning to a meeting to relive the past and escape the opportunity for change that exists in the present.

You're escaping yourself every day. Every damn day.

I've seen others go through this, including myself. I know it's no simple task to figure out why you are the way you are. However, that doesn't mean it has to be hard either. In AA they'll tell you that it's a lifelong battle and that you have to suppress your urge to drink at all times, but deep down, you and I both know that's not true. As to these "reasons" you drink, you've gotta understand that all you're doing is lying to yourself. Hiding from yourself. It may be deep down inside you. Or maybe you haven't figured it out yet. It may take you weeks, months, or years, or, heck, it might just take you a few hours. I've seen it happen before. It's really up to you. It begins once you start calling yourself out on the lies and the side of crap you've been feeding yourself every day, right along with your morning eggs.

That's where the transformation begins.

CHAPTER 11

TANGENT: AL-ANON

If you're not familiar with Al-Anon, think of it as a place for people who want to bitch and moan about something, but instead of it being their own addiction, it's the addiction of someone they care about. Like AA for people who really have nothing better to do.

If we're being honest, the program is laughable in itself. Of course it's hard to see your son getting high every day or your husband coming home plastered every night. But listen, sweetheart: this is not your life! It's also not your fault. So why on earth would you waste your time sitting around and moping about the behavior of someone else? No matter how much you love a person, they make their own choices. In this case, you actually are completely powerless! No amount of intervening or venting about it is going to change that. Sure, you might be able to suppress some of the pain. But where is that going to get you? At best, it might get you through one more day if you take it one day at a time. But if you've read this far, you already know what I think about that.

And look, I know that if someone you love is addicted to drugs, you share the same fear that everyone who knows and loves addicts shares: you're afraid of them dying. Driving off a cliff or running straight into another car and killing themselves or someone else. Choking on their own vomit. Snorting so many lines that they OD.

Hell, I know all about that.

> **FRAGMENT—LATE-NIGHT DRIVES**
>
> I've been chasing the pipe for god knows how many days now. I love the feeling of my late-night drives, singing at the top of my lungs to my favorite CDs and driving with no destination in mind. I'm starting to hallucinate as I'm going eighty down the interstate. I see Zeus appear in the sky with his massive lightning bolt, stabbing down from the clouds trying to stake my coupe. I weave frantically back and forth across the freeway trying to dodge him.

That was a fun day.

And I get it. You might think this is funny now. At the time that shit felt so real that I ended up on the side of the road with my knees tucked into my chest as I sat on the ground in the pitch black of night, rocking back and forth in paralyzing fear. And for the people who cared about me during that period, those drives put me inches from making that nightmare come true.

The bottom line is that deep down, you aren't really all that mad about your son getting kicked out of school or your husband passing out on the floor of his man cave again. You're afraid that if you don't step in now, if you don't do something, they are going to continue spiraling to their death.

In truth, there's only one real answer here—and you're not going to like it. The only real answer for how to deal with your loved one being an addict is to accept that you cannot change them. You can't. You can spend your time and energy trying to change them, but it just won't work. The addict has to wake up one day and decide they truly want to change. They are ready to begin the process of transforming from the addict self, the old self, to the new version of themselves that they want to become. That's it.

"But May," you ask, "what if they refuse to change? What if they continue drinking or doing drugs?" The answer is simple, although hard to swallow: move the fuck on. If this makes you feel guilty, ask yourself whether the bad behavior of another person is worth damaging the quality of your own life. If it makes you feel like you're giving up on them, ask yourself what you would want your loved ones to do if the roles were reversed. Should you allow the actions of another person to destroy your life along with theirs? I didn't think so. Give what you can, but ultimately look out for yourself and make it clear that *if* that person is really ready to make a change, you'll be there for them.

Karma means destiny or fate. A fellow Buddhist once said to me, "Never disrupt anyone's karma." Because yes, you can lend a helping hand and point them in the direction of their destiny, but that person still has to walk toward it. This is regardless of whatever expectations you might have because everyone creates their own cause and effect. So stop trying to control their outcomes.

At the end of the day, you have to do what's best for you. If this means divorcing your alcoholic spouse, then call your lawyer and file the paperwork. If it means saying goodbye to your best friend, make the call. I'm not saying you have to be harsh; your compassion and love for the person are what makes this so damn hard in the first place. But if this is a person who doesn't appear to be willing to change in the near future, cut the cord and surround yourself with people whose presence in your life will offer the positivity and support that you deserve.

CHAPTER 12

THE REPETITIVE DANCE

If you're living your life following the same set of patterns, you are, by definition, not breaking any of the patterns that define your current way of living. So by going to AA meetings, calling sponsors, and going through the 12 Steps over and over, there's no endpoint to your journey as an addict in recovery. So, therefore, there is no end.

When you really think about it, AA is just like going to school but never graduating. In school, you learn something new, and you pass a test, and then you move on to the next grade. After all, you're not supposed to repeat kindergarten every year, are you?

What if, instead of continuing on with the same set of patterns and behaviors that have kept you on the brink of falling back into addiction, you decided to break those patterns and create new ones? What if you traded negative AA meetings filled with addicts for a group that does something you're actually passionate about—one that's filled with positivity and inspiration? What if instead of constantly looking into the past, you created the kind of patterns that the best version of your future self would have? What do you think your life would look like then?

Over time, I was able to overcome my negative patterns through a lot of deep self-work and dedication. I observed many people around me deciding to be lazy and give into the same old, same old. Whether for better or worse, we create the patterns and programs that dictate what our lives will look like.

What kind of patterns do you want to define yours?

CONCLUSION

Most people buy into the "consensus" that AA is the best and straightest path toward overcoming addiction. To me, AA looks like a gigantic squiggly road with infinite obstacles, twists, and turns. Every time you think you've conquered the biggest hill, all you can see in front of you is more mountain. This is why 90–95 percent fail. And for the 5–10 percent who "succeed," the reality is that despite the road starting to feel smoother and straighter over time, they don't realize that it never ends. And without them realizing it, their entire life becomes the ride.

In my vision of addiction recovery, I picture a straight and narrow road with a couple of massive Evel Knievel–style motorcycle jumps. You gear up, face them head-on, and take the leap. Then you hop off your bike, go for a walk, and smell the roses, and you're finally home.

PART II

OLD SELF TO NEW SELF

BREAKING THE RULES

If you are serious about recreating yourself, I'll be honest with you: you have some work ahead of you. Some of it will be hard. Some of it will be shockingly easy, and at times it will feel surprisingly satisfying. But the most important thing to remember is this: by finally deciding to let go of your old self, you are taking a real step toward changing yourself and your life. Not an arbitrary step written by a guy who lived 100 years ago. But a real, tangible first step that is rooted in a commitment to doing your own self-work.

And remember, you can simultaneously have respect for your old self and admiration for your new self. In the present moment, right here, right now, you can vow to change your life. No more hamster wheels. No more repetitive one-day-at-a-time bullshit. This isn't about anyone else but *you*. It's about the choices you make from here on out as if nothing else matters. Because nothing matters more than *you*.

It's time to cut out the excuses, lies, rules, and any other BS you've sold yourself on.

To commit to doing the self-work to carve out the life you want to live.

To create the person you *actually* want to be.

CHAPTER 1

THE OLD SELF

I'm almost positive this isn't the life you imagined for yourself. Waking up with a needle sticking out of your arm, vomit on your shirt, empty booze bottles all around. Not knowing where you are. Not recognizing the half-naked person lying next to you. Not even knowing what day it is. I'm willing to bet you never dreamed of a life where you woke up hungover and jonesing for a pipe. I obviously don't know you personally, but I'm fairly confident you've never woken up and said, "Last night was amazing. I don't remember a thing—what a life I have!"

For addicts, one of the major parts of moving from the old self to the new self is to free yourself from the Anonymous methodology. Without doing so, you're going to find yourself in the same old cycles you've spent all this time trying to escape.

If you're currently an addict, that sucks. If you're actively abstaining from being an addict, that sucks too. But if you are still telling yourself that you don't want to become "clean," or you have doubts about whether you actually want to be "sober," go ahead and crawl back into whatever hole you have dug and stay there until you're ready to come out and join reality. Because if you truly believe the best version of your life is having your body filled with toxins and your mind filled with regret and shame, who am I to judge?

> **FRAGMENT—THE MORNING OF MY AWAKENING**
>
> I wake up and look up at my popcorn ceiling. I have a popcorn ceiling? How have I never noticed that before? I look around. I see my pipe lying on the floor, blackened and empty. I lift up my alarm clock where I hide my baggies. Damn. Empty too. What the fuck happened? I remember being so high that I didn't sleep for seven nights straight. I must have blacked out. How long has it been? Where did everyone go? And what day is it?
>
> I rub my eyes, confused. I grab my phone to check. It's Sunday. That means I've been out for over two days.
>
> Jeez. What else did I miss?

This is one of the many reasons I don't have any interest in returning to my old self. When people in AA fall back into addiction, they aren't aware of the time they are wasting. Not just doing drugs but participating in all of it—from the painfully boring meetings to the interactions with their pathetic and helpless sponsors. So they just keep going. For me, I'm able to go about my life with a sense of ease because I can look back at my years of addiction, chalk it up to a past experience, and move on. Over and out.

I get that it's different for everyone, but excuse me for pointing out the obvious that looking within is the only way to make real changes. Instead of trading my addiction for other means of coping, I put myself on a journey toward overcoming myself. I laughed off the idea of placing my health and "sobriety" in the hands of a sponsor, or anyone else for that matter. I found tools that worked for me and focused on moving on. Away from the dogma of relapsing and recovery. Away from living life in the past. Away from all the bullshit.

And through that, I began to grow.

CHAPTER 2

CALENDARS VS. GROWTH

In AA, they often say that time heals all.

Does it, though?

To me, it seems like self-work and prioritizing your ability to overcome yourself are a better recipe for paving a path toward the person you want to become. The 12-step programs teach us to focus on staying "clean" and "sober" one day at a time. Sure, it sounds all right. But there's no future in it. They tell you that you will never *not* be an addict. You will always have to surrender. You'll always be working through the steps. You'll always have to attend meetings. As the saying states, "Energy flows where your attention goes." If you place all your attention on counting days of "recovery" until your next "relapse," then that's exactly where you're headed.

CALENDARS

In AA, you're taught to buy yourself a calendar and cross off every day that you don't use. The idea is that through the daily repetition of crossing off your days, you will create both a literal and psychological chain of progress that will help you resist the urge to break that chain.

Here's the problem with this: the day-by-day, calendar-based approach is just like everything else you might do in AA. **Keeping a calendar isn't going to lead you to a new life; it's just marking off the days you're not fully living.** Being fully alive means to be living in the present moment. Not counting the days you've been "sober." If you're truly "sober," you don't need a clock ticking. There is no more clock. You've defeated the monster, and you've moved on to the next chapter. If you take a step back and think about it, it's pretty obvious that there are other ways you could use the concept of time to your advantage. Getting stuck in your past is a real thing. So is defining a vision of your future, which we will discuss more in a bit. But it is important to realize that one of the ways AA brainwashes you with their propaganda is through this subtle but very real aspect of their philosophy: if you want to stay "sober," then you have to do things their way.

You have to make amends.

You have to put your faith in a higher power.

You have to accept their belief that recovery is a lifelong process.

They tell you to do things their way and to obey their rules. All 12-step programs teach a copy-and-paste timeline that is designed for everyone. They tell you to buy a plant so you can learn how to be responsible for something other than yourself. If that plant is still alive in a year, you're ready to own a pet! And if you manage to not kill that pet, then maybe, just maybe, you are ready for a real-life romantic relationship. According to AA, everyone needs to be coddled with the same trivial bullshit timeline because everyone is the same.

This way of thinking is flawed in more ways than one. For example, I could sit here and give you the same type of instructions based on the practices I believe in.

Hey, you!

You have to meditate.

You have to journal.

You have to become a spiritual person.

Are these things helpful? Yes. But if you feel forced into doing them, they're not going to work. Instead of being a good little girl or a good little boy and doing as you are told, turn your focus inward and ask yourself some honest questions. What things will best serve me? What habits can I create that will make me feel good? What do I want my future to look like—and what do I need to do in order to get there? And what are my beliefs around being worthy enough to achieve it?

Take a moment and consider these things. Grab a pen and scribble some ideas in the margins, or take notes in your Kindle. Think about what sort of things you like to do. No, not the ones you're *supposed* to do—I mean the ones that really make your heart flutter. This might be doing the things you love most or going and trying things you have always wanted to do but haven't yet. You know what I'm talking about. For some, the ultimate goal might be to overcome their addiction and become a NASCAR driver. In that case, that person should go full Ricky Bobby and ditch the toy Barbie car. Shake and bake, baby!

Your desires may be entirely different. The important thing to remember is that people whose activities aren't fixated on ruining their own lives are actually partaking in and contributing to our society. You may not want to go to space, create apps, open a law firm, or even be a barista. You have your own path, your own dreams. That's what makes us so unique and separates us from one another. That's why we were all born diversified. No one can force a cookie-cutter lifestyle onto you, not your friends, parents, AA, or anyone else. Just because one way doesn't work for you *does not* mean that you should just keep being an addict.

"Well, since I wasn't able to keep these orchids alive, and I'm not allowed to have sex, and I somehow lost interest in these plastic chips my sponsor keeps handing me…I guess I'm just stuck being an addict for the rest of my life."

Take a second and consider how that sounds when you say it out loud.

Do yourself a favor and cut out all the noise. Take some time to figure out what *actually* resonates with you. Be patient with yourself. If all you've been doing for the past five years is teetering between getting drunk at dive bars and struggling through meetings, it might take some experimenting to find the things that speak to you. But once you do—and you will—you will soon find yourself tossing your sobriety calendar in the trash and turning your attention to something much more exciting: your growth.

GROWTH

It's funny how most people are not using the day-by-day method correctly. Living day by day in the present moment is about embracing the human experience. In AA, taking it "one day at a time" means eventually arriving at the same destination you were headed for all along: "relapse."

But what if the process is different for everyone? What if it's all a choice? You can spend the rest of your time on this planet suppressing your emotions. Or you can decide to change and never look back. It really is up to you. You can look at life as a thing you take one day at a time. Or you have the option to pave your life one brick at a time. Because that way you're no longer living a life of running from the past—you're paving a way toward your future.

In the book *The Four Agreements* by Don Miguel Ruiz, there is a story that directly points at this innate human truth. A man asks his Buddhist teacher how long it will take him to gain enlightenment if he meditates four hours per day. The teacher replies, "Maybe ten years." The man then asks how long it will take if he meditates eight hours per day instead. "Maybe twenty," replies his teacher. The man looks at his teacher, confused, and says that he does not understand. The teacher gently explains that with all the precious time the student is willing to sacrifice in order to gain enlightenment, he doesn't realize the joy that is available to him in the present moment.

As they say, enlightenment isn't something that is achieved over a lifetime of study but instead is something available to us moment to moment. The same is true for your addiction. You can spend the rest of your life in a state of suffering and struggle to attain some elusive goal. Or you can choose to see the power in your current state and the beauty in the vision you could create.

You don't need a group with an arbitrary set of rules and steps to get to where you want to be. You can become the new you just by analyzing the choices you made in the past and recognizing the changes you want to make in the future. For example, let's say the thing you want most is a life partner, but you recognize that you currently have an issue with codependency. The AA method would tell you that you need to complete the tried and true 12 Steps before you can change.

But what if all you actually need to do is to sit down and spend some time deeply analyzing where your codependency stems from? What if after four days, or three weeks, or two months, you are able to work through your issues, understand where they come from, and update your frame of mind to no longer let your past trauma or fear of abandonment dictate your future relationships?

You are in charge of your own life, and I know that may sound like a burden, but trust me—it's an opportunity.

CHAPTER 3

SPONSORS VS. COACHING

Now let's address one of the most rib-tickling (and dangerous) aspects of AA: sponsors.

Sponsors are not qualified to help you or anyone else struggling with addiction. I mean, who thought it would be a good idea to have someone who is broken try to fix someone else who's broken? Most sponsors haven't worked through their core problems either. Which means when it comes time for them to give their sponsee advice, the best they can do is to project onto them what they think based on their own misguided experience. **Now that's what I call a classic case of copy and paste.**

SPONSORS

Let me ask you this: if a sponsor has been "sober" for five, ten, or twenty years, why are they still there? Why are they unable to let go of their past selves and *actually* move on? I sure as fuck have! The truth is that they, like everyone else in AA, live in a constant state of fear. AA conditions people to feel like without having AA in their lives, they will ultimately "relapse." So out of fear, people dedicate a few hours a week for the rest of their lives to this program that has brainwashed them into a never-ending loop.

It's like a bunch of people going around peacocking, saying, "Look at me," with puffed-up chests, as if we should put them on a pedestal for marking off another day in their calendar. It's laughable, really. Why would I want to be anything like them? They believe they're truly not struggling anymore, so they mask their own temptations by veering their attention away from their own problems of addiction and professing a bunch of mumbo jumbo.

They tell you that you constantly have to work at it, but it's only constant work if you still haven't let go of the reason you started using it in the first place. Umm…duh, remember? That's called suppression.

When it comes to advice, you have to realize that sponsors are either projecting or reciting the Big Book. You see, sponsors don't exactly have the deepest bag of tricks to begin with because everything they've been taught in AA is so washed down. One person's advice turns into another person's advice, and so forth.

Remember the telephone game we played when we were kids? You know, the one where the class gets in a big circle and each person whispers a message to the person next to them until it makes its way back to the person who went first? Boy oh boy, we used to get such a kick out of this game because what ended up being revealed in the end was always so different from what was originally said.

The sponsor program is dangerous for the same reason. Sponsors themselves aren't accredited counselors, therapists, or addiction recovery coaches. They're just taking some clichés they overheard in meetings and messages they were told by their sponsor and regurgitating them back to you. It's like a giant hundred-year-long game of telephone that started with Bill W and has now made it all the way back to you.

Is this really the message you want to base your future on?

HIGH RISK, LOW REWARD

It's easy to break down why sponsors aren't the best people to look to for advice. But what most people don't realize is that the risk of relying on your sponsor is bigger than it might seem.

For one thing, sponsors are just regular people with their own problems. No matter how caring or kind they may be, eventually your sponsor is going to get tired of hearing you cry wolf all the time.

"Help me. I'm two seconds away from the liquor store."

"I couldn't help it. I called my drug dealer, and he's on his way over."

"I just opened a bottle of wine. I'm falling off the wagon."

At first your sponsor will try to be there for you. They'll hit you with their go-to lines.

"Just resist, man!"

"You'll ruin everything you've worked toward!"

"Don't do it or you'll have to start back over on day one!"

If you start depending on your sponsor as the only barrier between you and your so-called "relapse," then eventually your sponsor is going to run out of ideas and patience. They will no longer be able to keep you on the wagon. **Their "great advice" will start to lose its potency.** Are you starting to see what I mean when I say that no one else can solve your problems for you? As we'll talk about later, coping is just a temporary fix. Relying on a sponsor is just another method of coping.

In truth, this isn't even the most dangerous part. The real danger in relying on a sponsor is that placing all your trust in this person makes you vulnerable. What happens if one day they are no longer able to be there for you? For example, imagine that you are on the verge of a "relapse," and you call your sponsor, and they don't pick up. You reach for the bottle, and just before the glass hits your lips, your phone rings. Phew! Your sponsor was there to save the day and walk you off the ledge once again. Hallelujah!

But what if the same thing happens eight days later, and your sponsor doesn't call you back? If you're caught in this pattern, there's a good chance you'll slide right back into your cycle.

Even worse, what happens if your sponsor goes through a major life transition of their own? What if their wife leaves them or they lose their job, and they decide to just say, "Fuck it," and get wasted? If you've been following their rules and going along with the program, seeing a sponsor or someone else in the group "relapse" will start to mess with your mind. This person you've been looking up to has fallen off their pedestal. Their cape has now been ripped off their hero costume. You start to think that if your sponsor can "relapse," then anyone could. And if that's true…what's stopping you from "relapsing" too?

This is reality folks. I should know.

> **FRAGMENT—LATE 2000S**
>
> Is that…Viktor? Holy shit, what's up, man! It's been at least two years since I've seen this guy. Viktor asks if I heard about Dave.
>
> Dave who? My old sponsor? What happened?
>
> They found him in his trailer. He overdosed on his eleventh sobriety birthday.
>
> Fuck.

This goes to show that at the end of the day, your sponsor can't be your savior. You have to be your own savior.

COACHING

Having a specialized addiction recovery coach is very different from having a sponsor. Sponsors, much like lifelong unaccredited therapists, focus on the past. They keep you stuck in the loop of your habitual cycles.

Both specialized addiction recovery coaches and life coaches help you create a vision for the future. They help push you toward your desired outcome. They inspire you. They hold you accountable. Coaches help customize a plan for overcoming your addiction that accounts for your personal challenges *and* your individual strengths.

This transition from sponsor to coach gives you the ability to start thinking for yourself again, to make decisions that serve your ideal state of being and even unlock the answers to those core reasons you became an addict in the first place.

Coaches aren't going to prescribe a specific list of steps for you because, of course, there is no one-size-fits-all tool kit in the real world. We are all different. We all have different skills, different needs, different wants. I could tell everyone to do yoga and meditate, but that's probably not going to work for a biker dude named Tony who is stuck in a cycle of drinking cold ones with his biker gang at the bar every night.

Coaches will introduce you to a series of questions you can ask yourself to figure out what *you* really want. Remember, this isn't school, and there will be no exam at the end. Your coach, unlike a sponsor, isn't there to pat you on the back and give you an A for effort. You're not there to impress them. At the end of the day, you are the one who is going to be living your life.

THE DANGER OF STORIES

We all have stories that we tell ourselves. Dwelling on the same stories keeps people stuck in the past. Sponsors, much like lifelong therapists, live for those kinds of stories. They encourage you to keep digging deeper and deeper into the past, and before you know it, you've dug yourself in so deep that you can't see the light anymore. You've become addicted to the stories, the feelings, and the thoughts that reaffirm your beliefs. Spending all this time thinking about the past makes it impossible to create a better vision for the future. It's like digging your own grave.

Don't get me wrong. Inner work is important, and doing the work to reflect on your past can create these gratifying "aha moments" where you realize the root of your problem. The issue is that after this realization, people use the "aha moment" as an identity and an excuse to keep carrying their past around, to continue telling the same stories and excusing the same behaviors instead of using what they've learned to achieve a breakthrough. This is where most people get stuck.

It's also where a coach can help.

Your coach will want to hear your story too—but as a summary. And believe me. They're going to force you to skip the fluff and get straight to the stuff that matters.

"So a couple of years ago, on a Tuesday morning at 7:52 a.m., I got out of bed, and I made coffee. I got in my car—it was a green Saab passed down to me from my grandfather. I was upset and running late to work. I remember this day because my astrology app said that…"

Your coach picks up the TV remote and points it at your face. "Let's go ahead and fast forward through the nonsense and get to what you're *really* trying to say. What exactly in this story is triggering you? How can you become aware of this trigger and dismantle it? What would it take for you to let go of this story? And how can you create space for new beliefs and happier stories?"

Like I said before, a coach isn't there to hold your hand. A coach has no interest in letting you waste an entire hour on a story that has a high emotional charge but no actual relevance to your goals. Your coach knows damn well that reciting the same old stories has no positive effect on your future. There is only one useful purpose of constant reflection on the past, which is to find the common denominators between your stories. This is how you find your patterns, which is how you figure out what makes you tick.

A coach will challenge you to look for answers to the questions that really matter. What do you actually want? It's not a chip. It's not a sobriety birthday. What is it really? Seriously, ask yourself what gets you excited to get out of bed in the morning. What obstacles are in the way of you doing more of that? At our core, the big question we're asking ourselves is this: what do I need to do to let the person I want to become shine? Coaches will continue pushing you toward your ultimate outcome—becoming the person you want to be—and helping you find the stepping stones you need to get there.

The vision of the Anonymous program doesn't include this kind of future. It's funny. People in AA will say, "Wait a sec…I've completed the 12 Steps, but I don't feel any different than when I first started the program. I'm not healed. I haven't overcome my addiction. Where's Step 13? And what's the solution?" Because in AA they treat addiction like a lifelong journey. Like monitoring a baby who is constantly whining for his pacifier.

A journey with no end.

People who go to a coach after coming from 12-step programs can sometimes start to rely on their coach the same way they were conditioned to rely on their sponsor. I want to be very clear: your coach is not your sponsor. Once again, you're grown. Start acting like it. Your coach isn't here to pull you from the ledge. Your coach is there to strengthen your ability to self-actualize. Take it from Tom Hanks in *A League of Their Own*: "Are you crying? There's no crying in baseball!" We're in the big leagues now.

I want you to imagine that you are in a dark cave that has a series of forks in the road. Which path do you choose? And who do you trust to lead you in the right direction? A good coach is like Indiana Jones, and you work together to try to find your way out. Your instincts may be telling you to go down the same paths you always take, the ones that keep you telling the same old stories and repeating the same old behaviors. Your coach is there to hold up a torch and point you in the direction that leads you out of the cave.

At the end of the day, a coach will force you to face yourself in the present. A coach is in the bleachers rooting for you to keep searching, saying, "Cheers to your future!" while holding up a glass of apple cider. Unlike a meeting leader who will always say, "Great share—see you next week!"

Need a shoulder to cry on? Call your sponsor.

Feeling inspired and want to *actually* start changing your life? Call your coach.

CHAPTER 4

MEETINGS VS. SUPPORT

Let's draw a clear distinction between meetings and support.

Sitting in a circle with people who are struggling with the same thing you are is completely absurd. What makes you think Sally with the Xanax addiction is going to be able to help you overcome your weed addiction? Doesn't the saying go "Two wrongs don't make a right"? What you are doing here is venting. And sure, venting can be useful as a once or twice occurrence. Anything more than that is just wasting more of your time. Explain to me how you and Sally bitching about the negative things in life (or things you cannot change) is actually effective? What is this accomplishing?

Great. You got it off your chest. Let's move on.

Support, on the other hand, offers something invaluable to people working their way out of addiction. So why do most people still choose meetings over *actual* support? Oh right.

There's some self-work to be done, and nobody wants to do that, do they? Of course not. Let's just head to this meeting and continue bitching about why we can't change—or whatever lies you keep telling yourself.

MEETINGS

Going to AA is sort of like punching an impenetrable brick wall over and over and expecting to break through it (unless you're Bruce Lee, of course). I mean, how can anyone expect to restructure their life without disconnecting from the habits and ways of thinking that created the person they have been all along?

When you attend a meeting, you're spending your valuable time—frankly, an embarrassing amount of time—but you're not getting anything in return. You throw on your PJs and walk into some building for a cute little session of listening to bitching and moaning, followed by some bitching and moaning of your own. Then afterward, everyone walks out feeling accomplished. But what exactly was accomplished in that room? You sat around spinning your wheels and hitting all your emotional buttons for an hour? Was that a good investment of your time?

They tell you to blindly follow the 12 Steps without thinking any of it through on your own. For example, Step 4 instructs that you take a fearless inventory of yourself. In modern life, this step needs to be rewritten to reflect the question of not just what you've done but why you've done those things. Why are you acting this way? Where are these triggers coming from, and why do you keep silencing them? But here we are again, hanging out in meetings and trying to analyze a hundred-year-old notion of what overcoming addiction is supposed to look like.

Think about it this way: if I told you there were a bunch of women sitting around talking crap about their ex-husbands, would you say that they were proactively trying to move past their old relationships? Or rather, would it seem like after a year of venting about it, they were stuck in the past with no hope of moving forward? I mean, do you really think these ladies are focusing their minds on envisioning what they want in their next partner?

If you've ever attended a meeting (which I'm sure you have), have you ever thought about what's really going on in there? They like to call it sharing, but again, it's really just venting. The problem here is that once you do something over and over again, you end up getting stuck in the same cycle. It's the same concept for addiction. Congratulations. You have now become addicted to venting.

You'll often see folks go up to the podium and introduce themselves because apparently it's only okay to be yourself around a bunch of other fuck-ups. No offense. But yes very much so. They proceed by repeating the same sentences they've said a thousand times. You think, *Oh yeah, there goes Jim again. He was tormented as a kid on the playground, so now he gets drunk and starts fights at bars every time he gives into his rage.* Or *Oh yeah, that's Betty. Betty's husband left her because she liked wine and smoking several packs of cigs a day just a little too much. But the real reason she was drinking (and the reason she avoids speaking about it directly) is that she has lived a life full of self-loathing because she never got to be prom queen.* So these same people go up and tell their sob stories of being "clean and sober" for some odd years and preaching to the newcomers to "keep on coming back" to…what? To be just like them? Are they really such role models?

The worst part of this circle of sharing is that you get to have a room of people feeling sorry for you (which we all know you love), and soon you become addicted to being in "victim mode." Now you might as well get nice and comfy because you're officially stuck in, what I like to call, the *permanent recovery zone*. The place where addict behaviors get to live on forever, sponsored by the one and only AA meetings.

PERMANENT RECOVERY ZONE

Let's imagine you sprained your ankle. So you go to the hospital and ask how long it will be until you are fully recovered. Eight weeks? Twelve weeks? You look at the doctor in anticipation. The doctor turns around and smiles, hands you a cup of stale coffee, and says, "You will be in recovery for the rest of your life, which means you're just gonna have to take this thing *one day at a time*." I think it's safe to say that you would run (or should I say hobble) away from that nightmare of a doctor as fast as you could. Because the idea that you would need to spend the rest of your life recovering from a temporary injury is, to put it nicely, fucking insane. We all understand that when we have an injury, we get professional help (as needed) and then do what we need to do in order to complete the recovery process.

But in AA, there is no recovery process. It's this same never-ending cycle from now to eternity.

In fact, let's talk more about *the now*. Let's take a moment to predict your inevitable future if you maintain this mindset around "recovery."

Sit and think it over. What will your life look like if you continue thinking this way? Will you be able to move on from your addiction, or will your entire existence as a human being be dedicated to a series of bad decisions you made years ago?

SUPPORT

I could write an entire book on the problems with meetings alone, but you and I both have better things to do. One of the biggest things that I find people don't quite understand is that, by definition, when you go to a meeting with a bunch of people struggling with addiction, you're surrounding yourself with a group of people with the same low vibrational energy that you need to escape in order to change. If you notice, there's not exactly a ton of inspiration that comes from those rooms. Sure, a lot of the people are nice. But have you ever thought about finding, oh, I don't know, nice people who will uplift you instead of constantly bringing you down? That is the only way to win this game.

Because let's face it: this life is a game. Your game. You are the creator and the star player, and you get to choose how you play. If you choose to play by living in constant reliance on something outside of yourself—with teammates who are trying to drag you down with them—you'll stay in the never-ending loop of misery and suffering. If you choose to instead assemble a team of friends, family, and professionals who have what it takes to help you succeed, well, now we're getting somewhere.

Support isn't constantly having to rely on everyone else around you. Support is about gaining lessons and implementing them into your everyday life in order to finally self-actualize.

CHAPTER 5

RELAPSING VS. REWIRING

The concept of "relapsing" is a big one, so I'm going to cut straight to the chase: relapsing isn't what you think it is.

RELAPSING: A TICKING TIME BOMB

"Relapsing" is an idea that they teach you in AA to fool you into thinking that the meetings, sponsors, and chips you've been collecting are the only things preventing you from falling back into your addiction. Sponsors will tell you that if you "relapse," you'll have to start all over from day one.

As if their program defines where you are at in your journey.

Let me ask you seriously: did you really not get any wiser in the meantime? This is probably not a question to be asking a chip. It's a question to ask yourself. What have you been doing the whole time you weren't using? Were you stuck in a state of suppression? If so, you probably didn't get any wiser. But what if you worked on yourself, and then you did end up "relapsing"—haven't you already made some progress? Or if you have multiple "relapses," isn't that also wisdom?

People often treat it like if you don't continue coming to meetings, you will inevitably "relapse" as a result. When is the wizard going to be unveiled behind this curtain, and why am I on this yellow brick road to nowhere? Once you see what's behind the curtain, you realize that the wizard isn't real. And neither is "relapsing."

Your participation in some arbitrary meetings does not determine your ability to "get clean" or become *pure*. This seems obvious. So why don't we question it? For addicts, AA seems to work like a short-term reset—AA uses the idea of relapsing as a mechanism to try to keep you "sober." But once again, that way of thinking keeps you trapped in the past. The answer lies in your ability to move on. Instead of playing their little games, be an adult and take an honest look at your life.

This is not to say that my journey was free of any kind of struggle. There were a lot of ups and downs for me in the midst of changing, and I actually did have a "relapse" toward the end.

FRAGMENT—4TH OF JULY, 2004

I've been sober for seventeen months now. I've been going to meetings for about three, ever since I met Viktor. I'm currently on Step 5. I'm hanging out at a Fourth of July party in San Francisco with everyone from the NA group, and I get a call from a guy named Greg. Huh, that's weird. I haven't heard from Greg in years. I pick up the phone. Within seconds I hear the clicking in his jaw and feel a switch flip inside of me.

Greg, where are you?

I make up a lie and tell my sponsor that I have to go, and he insists on riding the train with me back to my car. This is awkward. I can't wait to get away from this guy.

Now it's midnight, and I'm on the road to San Luis Obispo. That's where Greg lives. I keep looking at my maps—it says it's a five-hour drive, but my foot is pressing the accelerator as far down as it can go. I call up Greg and ask, "Where are you exactly?" He's at a friend's house. I say, "Listen very carefully: I'm gonna walk in. I'm not gonna say hi to your friend. I'm not gonna say hi to you. I want you to pack my pipe just the way I like it. I'm gonna sit down next to you, and you're gonna hand me the pipe. I'm going to take at least two hits. Then I'm going to wait one minute, and then I will say hi to you, and I will introduce myself to your friend."

Now it's about an hour from sunrise, and I'm walking into Greg's friend's house. I sit down on the couch next to Greg, and he hands me a pipe. His friend sits quietly in a recliner across from me. I look down and say, "Well, there goes seventeen months."

And then I take a hit.

You often hear people say, "I couldn't have done it without AA or NA." And that's fine. I can't speak for you or for anyone else. What I can say from my experience is that thanks to NA, I ended up "relapsing." Without NA, I would never have been programmed to think like the Anonymous program in the first place.

But the truth is that this single "relapsing experience" *did not* mean that all the inner work I did suddenly went away.

Picking up where we left off in "Sponsors vs. Coaching," what is your trigger? Locate it. Acknowledge it. Understand what is causing it. Then place your awareness on it to help you see the truth of the situation.

Once you've overcome your triggers, focus on the future instead of getting lost in arbitrary dates or sobriety chips because if you don't, you will inevitably fall back into your old ways. Why do you think people "relapse" after years or decades of sobriety? It's because on some level, we all see through the trivial nature of collecting chips or marking off days on the calendar. The "one day at a time" mantra becomes so overused that you no longer give a fuck about sticking to it.

The thing about drugs and alcohol is that they create a false reality.

"Yeah, no shit, May. That's why I wanna be there!"

You can tell yourself that taking another hit or having another drink is going to make you feel better. Ha. But you know damn well that as soon as you sober up, you will recognize that the only thing you accomplished was wasting more of your fucking time. You'll realize that your drugged-up state is *fake* and all you've done is pushed pause on your life. All your problems are still there. Be aware that as you start to sober up mentally (no pun intended), the cold, hard truth will start to creep in. You won't be able to stand the fake feelings or the lies you've been telling yourself. You'll be forced to finally face the person you have become.

For some, this false reality they've created is a result of negative emotions. Resentment is about not getting your way in the past. Anger is about not getting your way in the present. And worry is about not getting your way in the future. It's this worry and fear of the future that trips people up as they try to create this new version of themselves.

THE ART OF LETTING GO

Did you know that it's common for people in AA to "relapse" on their one-year anniversary of sobriety? If you didn't know any better, you might be surprised by this fact. I sure as hell wasn't. By definition, the anniversaries and "sobriety birthdays" are arbitrary dates used to incentivize people to resist the urge for just one more day. To stave off the demons they are refusing to face because their big one-year, five-year, or twenty-five-year sobriety birthday is coming up, and they sure don't want to fuck it all up before they get there.

The problem is that once they do hit those milestones, they get this amazing feeling of accomplishment. Unfortunately, this doesn't last long. Soon after, they begin to ask the inevitable question: "Now what?"

And it's a fair question. They've been good little Anonymous disciples and hit their made-up milestones. Maybe they call their sponsor or make a post on social media. But that's when reality hits—they don't have anywhere else to go. They've built their approach to recovery around gathering quick hits of praise from others and feeding their "victim mode" mentality. So they drink. They use. They throw it all away. **By basing their approach to sobriety on the 12-step model, they have given themselves no real future to strive toward.**

This concept brings to mind a story from Eckhart Tolle in his book *A New Earth*. In the story, two monks are on a pilgrimage, and they encounter a young woman who is attempting to cross a river with a strong current. The woman asks for their help, and despite the fact that these monks took a vow to avoid contact with women, the older monk picks the woman up and carries her across the river. A few hours later, the younger monk looks at the older monk in disbelief and says, "Brother, our spiritual training teaches us to avoid any contact with women, but you picked that one up and carried her!"

The older monk replies, "I set her down hours ago. Why are you still carrying her?"

Now I'll ask you the same question: You had a moment where you "relapsed." Why are you still carrying it around with you?

WITHDRAWAL

So far I've talked about how the decisions and choices we make determine everything in our lives. How you can't continue blaming your addiction or personal failures on things outside of your control. Not on your circumstances. Not on your trauma. Not on any of it.

What this means is that in order to create the life you want for yourself, you have to take accountability for getting out of your current situation and onto the path you want to be on. No more white-knuckling it. It's time to do it the right way. However, if you are in the beginning of your journey to becoming *pure*, your body may take some time to get on the same page as your newly awakened mind. If you're already past this stage, you will understand why I have to emphasize this point.

Just because you have made the decision to quit being an addict doesn't mean that your body will simply submit to that sudden shift. Know that you're the one who trained your body to have these cravings. Give yourself what you need. If you need to take a break and sleep for a week, do it. Let your body sit and ache and long for what it's been conditioned to crave. Acknowledge it. Don't feed it; feed on it. Recognize it for what it is: your body is screaming at you for a substance that you've let grab hold of you for the past however long you've been using. Become aware that your body, much like a child, is angry at you for taking away its little treat. But soon it will be thanking you. You see, these feelings of withdrawal are your body's way of letting you know that it has entered fight-or-flight mode. That it's trying to save you. Without substances, our bodies are working for us, not against us. By doing drugs, you are the one disrupting the natural process of your body.

Now it's your time to save your body. And your mind. And your soul. It's time for the big fight—break out those boxing gloves and get ready to brawl. In these first few weeks, imagine you're in the ring, and your addiction is going to keep throwing haymakers until you defeat it. But once you've won—once you've gotten through the withdrawal period and are moving on toward your new life—turn your back on that old motherfucker and never look back.

MAPPING

Most people are unaware of what's actually happening inside their own bodies. I mean...I guess it's fair to say that not everyone is fascinated by neuroscience. When past events trigger you and you begin to relive the experiences in your mind, your body isn't able to tell the difference between what you're experiencing in the present moment and the stress-induced response of the event you are recalling from the past. Be aware of the fact that your mind, body, and spirit are experiencing the effects of a chemical reaction in your brain to create the emotion you are feeling. It's not some inescapable force that you are trapped inside; it's simple biology. The trigger causes your dopamine levels to rise, and by association, your desire for the substance is activated.

When this happens, the Anonymous way of doing things features an adorable little set of coping mechanisms. These keep your mind running the same program and, from a physiological level, do not give your body the chance to escape the loop.

When we leave addiction behind and begin growing into our new selves, we realize that we actually find comfort in the hurt. We find comfort in the pain. We lean on our pain body (an accumulation of old emotional wounds that can suddenly reactivate) not because it feels good but because of what we get as a result. Recognizing this pain body as an energetic echo of past traumas allows us to separate it from our true selves. So instead of battling the feeling of the unknown, we are able to finally find an answer to the pain. To associate that pain with a victory of growth in our own character, which feels really fucking good.

REWIRING

With your old self in the past, it becomes time to rewire your mind and figure out what you *actually* want to do with your life. Pretty soon you will stop worrying about what some sponsor or Anonymous group will say because you'll be too busy actualizing yourself. Best of all, you don't have to wait until you achieve what you're trying to do in order to feel satisfaction and see the benefits of your growth. The simple act of having a vision (one that is based on what you really care about, not some bullshit your parents or society set out for you) and working toward it is one of the most gratifying things in life.

When it comes to rewiring your brain, here's how it works: place awareness over what thought is being fired. Question what's triggering it. Understand where the thought comes from, and then dismantle it by reframing the negative thought with a positive one. This is how you can begin breaking down your negative thought patterns and start to see all the possibilities you've been missing.

TRANSITIONS

Don't get me wrong; this transition is different for everyone. Some find it difficult. For me, it was the easiest thing I ever did. The reason the transition can feel uncomfortable is it requires you to move away from a familiar feeling. Which is a good thing. Because if you're still feeling the same things, then you're probably heading toward a dead end. Feeling the same things leads to the same actions, which leads to the same results, which leads to you going around and around in circles until you finally decide to do something different. And if you never actually do anything different while expecting a different result, isn't that the definition of insanity?

And, hey, don't forget that when it starts to feel uncomfortable, that's a sign that you're heading in the right direction. That you've found a path that leads somewhere you actually want to go. So don't stop there. Keep going!

Discomfort can appear in different ways. Sometimes it's productive, but there are also situations where it's a complete waste of your time. You want to make yourself uncomfortable because you're changing for the better, not because you're torturing yourself to write down all the things you've ever done wrong. Like, oh, I don't know, Step 4?

If you really care about changing, I won't need to convince you. Instead of clinging to what's familiar, and instead of an arbitrary date or chip, the reason you will ultimately be able to change is that becoming your new self will be so much more enticing than continuing to stay the same.

Whether you are serious about taking ownership of your recovery—and putting what you learn in this book to work in a way that is personal to you—that's up for you to decide. If you really want it, you will find a way.

If you don't, it will inevitably be back to the bottle, pills, or pipe for you.

CHAPTER 6

COPING VS. OVERCOMING

Coping with and overcoming your addiction are two different things.

Coping is the Anonymous-approved way of dealing with addiction. It involves pacifying your desire to drink with quick hits of meetings, calls with sponsors, and that good ole feeling of superiority that comes from hearing the stories of people who are worse off than you.

Overcoming your addiction, on the other hand, is about addressing the root of the problem: addressing your ticks, addressing what you're suppressing, and dismantling the very parts of you that make you feel and think the way you do. As hard as it is, it takes you pushing yourself to overcome this enemy that is yourself. You hearing me yet?

Here's the truth: the way you think about dealing with your

addiction will play an important role in your ability to successfully transition out of your old self and into the new. If this is the case, why do so many people cope with their addiction—along with any other struggles they have in their lives—instead of focusing on overcoming themselves? It's because when they run into a trigger, they either "relapse" or cope with it. If you're wondering why people do this, it's because it's what they've been taught by the "experts." So they never think to look for option C.

COPING AND TRIGGERS

When you walk into a meeting, you are getting ready to do one of three things: listen to other people bitch about themselves, unconsciously numb out and check another meeting off your calendar, or, if you're in the mood to share, bitch about yourself. So week after week, you show up and talk about the things that triggered you over the past few days, and everyone in the room huddles together in hopes that they'll be able to hang on to their precious sobriety for just another week.

Frankly, this behavior is ludicrous.

When you call your sponsor and tell them that you were tempted by one of your triggers, they'll tell you to rely on your five lines of defense—calling a friend, going to a meeting, suppressing the urge, distracting yourself with something else, or perhaps another coping mechanism they've taught you. But, uh, where exactly do those coping mechanisms transition into solutions for overcoming these triggers?

Next time you face a trigger, trade out their five lame lines of defense for something more productive. Perhaps something like "five lines for giving yourself a chance." This could be centered around finding an addiction recovery coach, journaling on "what would you rather," utilizing tools to attack the root of the problem, or seeking advice from someone who has successfully overcome their addiction (and isn't stuck in the constant loop of going to meetings every week to talk about it). If all else fails, dig deep and ask the question that only you can answer for yourself: what do you truly need at this moment?

In the Introduction, I mentioned that there were a few experiences from my childhood that laid a foundation for my addictive behaviors. For one, I developed a massive fear of vomiting when I was a child. Anytime I ate a meal, I felt overwhelming paranoia that I was going to vomit. Same thing when I went to sleep—I was terrified of waking up and vomiting in the middle of the night. But I wasn't sure why. I figured out later that I was temporarily pacifying these triggers with my addiction to meth. Because if you think about it, what are two things meth does for virtually everyone who uses it?

It makes you not want to eat or sleep. Bingo! I had found my drug of choice.

What experience does your drug of choice give you? What personality traits are you trying to fake? Who are you pretending to be? Perhaps even more telling, what fears or anxieties does it take away? Once you identify those fears, tell me: why are you afraid of those things?

This doesn't mean that all addiction stems from childhood. You could have developed a way to protect yourself from an experience in adulthood as well. You took an experience or set of experiences and developed fears and anxieties around them to protect you from feeling those things again.

Either way, the process of overcoming your addiction remains the same.

OVERCOMING

The hardest thing for us humans is to change. To dedicate ourselves completely to avoiding seeking validation and pleasure from things outside of ourselves. Whether your life is good or bad is completely dependent on you and your beliefs, emotions, feelings, experiences, and immediate environment.

So when you feel triggered, reject the urge to cope. Avoid calling sponsors or preparing a speech for your next NA meeting. Face the trigger head-on and use the skills you learned in "Rewiring" to work toward the process of overcoming.

Whatever your situation may be, I promise you that there are deeper answers than you will find on your first look.

Push yourself to keep looking deeper.

Push yourself to overcome it.

CHAPTER 7

DENIAL VS. AWARENESS

> "We can deny reality, but we can't deny the consequences of denying reality."
>
> —RICHARD PAUL EVANS

DENIAL

Let's be honest: everyone who is addicted to drugs is in denial. Not just denial about how bad their drug problem is. Ha. That would be too easy. People are in denial that they're only addicted to the substance but not the real reasons behind it. The bottom line here is that you don't actually like yourself. You might say, "No, May, I love myself—I just also love doing drugs." Well, if that was the case and you truly liked yourself, why would you need to alter yourself to a point of disillusionment? You just sound silly.

Find me someone who truly loves themself; they won't need a thing to alter their current state of mind. Now that's true self-love. When you see people up at the podium giving their "I hit rock bottom" speech, some dork will always say, "Wow! Thank you for sharing." Ummm...why? Did they inspire you in some way? Do you wanna hit rock bottom too?

As you know by now, nothing gets accomplished in these situations, and you end up walking out of the meeting with your tail between your legs asking yourself, "How exactly is this serving me?"

Telling yourself that other people's stories are going to turn your life around is just another form of denial that is taking you further and further from the truth.

Denial isn't just something that we do as individuals. Heck, even some of the largest organizations in the world exist in a constant state of denial. Including, of course, AA. As I referenced earlier, there are parts of Bill W's story that most AA groups don't like talking about. While most people know that Bill had an awakening, the average AA-goer probably isn't as familiar with Bill's experimental LSD trips. Conveniently, that little detail got left out of the Big Book once AA became a worldwide phenomenon. It seems like their board members were so disgusted by him altering his mind with hallucinogens that they felt it would be better to just continue living in denial about who their leader really was.

THE WAY YOU WISH YOU WERE

Listen, if you want to sit around complaining about all the things you can't control, that's fine by me. Go ahead and waste the rest of the time you have on this planet reciting your steps and doing the outdated, redundant, merry-go-round homework they assign to you. But understand that you don't have to live like this. Some of the things you want might feel out of reach, but that's no reason to continue staying the same.

For example, let's imagine you're an out-of-shape, divorced, depressed man in his mid-forties, working a 9-to-5 that you hate, living in some shitty studio apartment somewhere in Suburbia, USA. Your ex-wife, your son, and your son's stepdad live in a nice house with a white picket fence across town. This is how your life is going right now.

Now let's say that deep down you've always fantasized about being a ripped surf instructor living in Hawaii. Not only have you convinced yourself that this is impossible, but because of your divorce and split custody of your son, you feel like you're going to be trapped in this town for the rest of your life because your ex-wife and her rich, handsome new husband are going to continue raising their family there. So now you feel like you are permanently stuck, and the only thing you look forward to is sucking down a twelve-pack every night to get you through the week until you can see your son on the weekend. Is there any way out?

Short answer: yes.

Longer answer: if it's not your dream to live in this shitty little town and this environment is making you hate life and feel worse about your current circumstances, it's probably not allowing you to show up as the best version of yourself in other parts of your life either. This is both good and bad. It's bad because you are very, very far from where you want to be in life.

It's good because by realizing this, you can give yourself permission to change. So let's imagine that you do.

Now fast forward six months. You've saved up money, quit your job, and moved to a cute surfer town in Hawaii. You quit drinking because you realized you were using alcohol to cover the shame for the ways you had been showing up as a father, which stemmed from your anger about your divorce. You work out seven days a week and are in the best shape you've been in since you were nineteen. You found an adorable little bungalow near the beach. You finished your certifications as a surf instructor and started a small surf school. You eat healthy and go about your day feeling strong and energetic. You met a lovely woman on the island and are happy waking up every day as the new you. You fly your son out to visit you, and he sees you as a new man, a happy man—one he begins to respect and admire. One he looks up to. He asks if he can spend the summers there with you. You work it out with his mother. This is how your life is going now.

Is this hypothetical version of yourself not a hundred times better than the way you used to be?

SELF-QUESTIONING

What would you rather? People often limit the questions they ask themselves to the surface-level things. And many others don't examine themselves at all.

1. What don't you like about yourself?
2. What stories do you keep telling yourself?
3. What do you believe you can't change?

4. Do you know what you would truly need in order to move on?
5. What do you want out of life?

Asking yourself these kinds of questions makes you realize that if you truly liked yourself, why would you feel the need to get intoxicated? Would drinking or doing drugs *really* be helping you reach your goals? These questions have the power to help you uncover what's at the core of your problems. But remember—this isn't going to work if you're just going to continue lying to yourself. You have to dig deep and speak your truth to find the answers you're looking for.

Once you begin this process, you'll continue diving deeper and deeper until eventually you find this thing called self-love!

AWARENESS

Being in denial about your addiction comes from believing that your addiction itself is your core problem, when you and I both know that's not true. By becoming aware of where the root of your problem actually lies, you give yourself the opportunity to change. And not only will this awareness help you face those core issues head-on, but it will free you to think bigger and start to figure out how you actually want to live your life.

Sometimes we dig holes for ourselves that feel impossible to climb out of. We never truly feel like these things we want are in our reach. This concept is at the core of how you can ask yourself what choices you would make as your new self. **Which would you rather do?** Make decisions that lead you to continue living this shitty life? Or get down in the trenches and crawl your way out?

My point here isn't to run away from your problems. My point is that you need to figure out what the *new you* looks like, even if the process of getting there makes things difficult in the short term. If you are sincere about wanting to change and you've put a plan in place to make it happen, the people in your life will understand. In fact, they'll probably be happy for you. There's nothing more inspiring than someone who actualizes the person they want to be. Especially when they have to overcome some adversity to get there. But this might not always be the case, so make sure you're always putting your own needs first.

This is an area of life that deserves so much of our time but is rarely given the attention it requires. Deep down, most addicts have some version of themselves that they would rather be, no matter how abstract that vision might look. Instead of letting those thoughts passively come and go, sit and write down what this person looks like. Write down the things you used to be and the way you used to think at the peak of your addiction. How do those compare with the way you *think* and *are* now? Be honest.

Next, write down the things you want to be as your new self. How would you describe yourself? What kind of thoughts are going through your mind? Are they toxic thoughts, full of complaints and excuses? Or are they positive, empowering thoughts focused on executing your vision for your life?

Perhaps most importantly, what are you looking forward to? Back when we were kids, we had so many things that we were excited about in the future, and this anticipation gave us life.

For many adults, it's been years since they had something to look forward to. Sad, right? Find something in your future that you are genuinely excited about. This is more about injecting some life into your soul and less about the event itself. This exercise will help you understand how to fall back in love with the journey of life.

Understanding the person you wish you were is an underrated way of figuring out who you want to become. By accepting your reality for what it is, you give yourself the chance to go out and get the things you want out of life.

CHAPTER 8

RELIGIOUS DOGMA VS. SPIRITUAL FREEDOM

I've said it before and I'll say it again—there are quite a few misconceptions when it comes to the origins of the Almighty Program.

DOGMA

You can be religious, spiritual, or nothing at all. Regardless, what you don't need to be is stuck in a rut reciting the 12 Steps and trying to save yourself. If you believe in God, great! This still doesn't mean that you get to cop out and "let go and let God." No. If you want to get through this, you're going to have to face your own inner demons before you can become the person you truly want to be.

While we're on the topic, if you do believe in God, do you really think he would want you to be constantly hitting him up and then running back to your loser friends to get high? Or to keep complaining about your temptation to get high?

As if God doesn't have better things to do.

Think about how the cryptic statements about "God" fool people into believing that the program is something different than what it was intended to be. As good of intentions as they might have had, the bottom line they were trying to convey is this: if you become a spiritual being, none of the things that made you an addict will be able to continue existing in your life. They will all magically fall away. To be honest, I can understand why this line of thinking might have made sense back then. But the messaging has gotten twisted in a way that makes it seem as though we are all powerless. We can just chalk it all up to God if we want to get better. The role of religion has become so misconstrued that no one understands it today. Which is why we're here.

In AA, they talk about God as a higher power. Have you ever asked yourself if they meant *a* higher power or *your* higher power? In modern times, we distinguish between these things. AA doesn't. AA says that the idea of a higher power, along with everything outside of us, is all God. If people in AA are asked about their thoughts on God, they answer with "whatever you believe that to be." Pretty convenient loophole, huh? So no matter what you tell them, they find a way to squeeze your beliefs into their cookie-cutter mold. **Because in AA, "God" can be anything. Well, anything but you.**

It's like they're deeply rooted in this idea of God but are trying to bend it and mold it to fit whoever comes through those doors. Rather than making use of science or more modern ways of thinking, AA has relied on the same fanatical ideas decade after decade. Were Bill W and Bob Smith really Christians? Doesn't matter. The argument is that you must rely on a higher power, which means whatever is *outside* of yourself that is more powerful than you! AA disciples will say that "God" could be the Christian God, Allah, Buddha, Jesus, the AA program, or the wisdom of the universe…so pretty much you could say your higher power is your dog. Give all your nonexistent power over to him, and have him howl it away! And as I said before, this is horseshit. Because you are the greatest power you will ever have.

No matter how little you bench.

The problem is that this approach is super disconnected from our real world. The "real world" may look different to all of us, but it's safe to assume that your world involves paying bills, having a roof over your head, building a career, and so on. If you're struggling with addiction on top of these other things, the power of this archaic way of looking at "getting clean" starts to lose its luster. This is an important point and a recurring theme in this book. Solutions to real-world problems that aren't based in reality will fall short when real life hits. Collecting sobriety chips sounds great until you miss a deadline at work and are feeling like shit after getting yelled at by your boss. Calling your sponsor after being tempted to use might be helpful until you log onto Facebook and see your ex with a new man. Him? Really?

And just like that, the fantasy is broken, and you're back to staring at the bottom of the bottle or sucking that joint right down to the end of its paper. Back to doing the same old shit that you hate yourself for ever doing in the first place. You (falsely) believe you can't face or fix your current reality. And you can't stand yourself either. So again you're faced with the "no way out" way of thinking. So you choose to escape it.

You have to understand that when you are programmed to recite the famous Serenity Prayer—"God, grant me the serenity to accept the things I cannot change, the courage to change the things I can, and the wisdom to know the difference"—what they're implying is that you can't change the fact that you are an alcoholic. And for the things AA tells you that you can change, those are usually just transitioning you from substance abuse to some form of coping, like distractions, meetings, sponsors, etc. The true wisdom lies in knowing the difference between the things keeping you in the past and the ones pushing you toward your future.

That is what the Serenity Prayer was originally intended for—long before it was corrupted by AA and used as a copout to *surrender* rather than find serenity.

It is so abundantly clear that this old-school way of thinking does not hold up when life puts us to the test. After all, if we must rely on God, meetings, and sponsors for everything, how could we expect to feel anything other than powerless? If you put two and two together, don't you see why you keep on choosing to "relapse"? Because when God isn't talking back and your life isn't panning out the way you imagined, who is the only person who can stand up and take charge? Umm...*you*.

That's why I prefer a new way of thinking. One where we are our own gods—because once we embrace that reality, how could we ever be powerless? If we take accountability and control over ourselves, then we understand that it's in our power to decide whether to pick up the pipe and smoke it. We get to choose whether to go to the liquor store or end up at the bar. These things are in our power. They have nothing to do with God and everything to do with us.

SPIRITUAL FREEDOM

I actually do believe in God and consider myself spiritual. I was born into the Jewish religion. Throughout my adulthood, I have had profound awakenings through my spiritual practice. In my early thirties, I also practiced Buddhism and Hinduism.

But that's not how I overcame my addiction!

Sorry for yelling. I just want to make sure I'm really clear about this. The bottom line is that religion has *less than nothing* to do with addiction. Zero.

We all carry traditions around with us. We are all reflections of things people said and did long before we were born. Back in the day, we had less of a choice of what to believe because there wasn't modern science to help us see life as we do today. Now that we've evolved as a species, we get to make our own choices. We can choose our religion and opinions. Heck, people can even choose their gender if they want to. But ultimately, it's your decision. And what is so powerful about this is that in embracing your ability to decide how *you feel*—no matter what other people think about it—you get to be free. Ah. Take a deep breath and think about how good it would feel to finally be free from the chains of what you're expected to believe. To let go of all of the things that don't serve you.

To have a life being totally pure and completely free.

I actually don't have too much else to say about your spiritual journey because at the end of the day, what you choose to believe is none of my business. Or anyone else's, for that matter. For me, spirituality helps me connect more deeply with myself, the world around me, and existence itself. But go on your own journey. Try out different things, and give your time and attention to whatever serves you best.

Just make sure it's on your own terms.

No matter what.

CHAPTER 9

SHAME VS. GRATITUDE

When you were a kid and people asked who you wanted to be when you grew up, was this it?

Time is running out quickly; I know you feel it too. We blink and suddenly three years have gone by. Hangovers and withdrawal are painful. But there's nothing worse than waking up and realizing you've wasted years of your life. Years you can never get back. If you are someone who's learned the same lessons over and over but continues to make the same mistakes, then that is all the more reason to commit to changing in a meaningful way. Lingering on mistakes you've made in the past simply ain't gonna cut it.

SHAME

You probably have shame you've been carrying around for a long time now. Shame for the things you wish could take back—the things you wish you could undo, the scenarios you wish you could change, the regrets you just can't unswallow. You might hate yourself even more when you realize how much you've been missing out on because you're too busy walking through life with your head in the clouds.

This might sound hard to believe, but when I look back on my past, I don't feel any shame. Because as you'll learn, carrying around shame will only make things harder.

Have you considered the possibility that instead of all this shame and self-hatred, you could actually feel…oh, gosh, I don't know… gratitude? You've had this experience where you've now hit the lowest of lows, and as a result, you finally realize that you're ready to change. Because if you weren't ready to change, you wouldn't be here, reading this book.

So you might be wondering, "May, where does the gratitude kick in?" It kicks in when you realize that when it comes to addiction, there aren't any scenarios where future use will serve your life in a positive way.

GRATITUDE

With this realization comes the first building blocks toward change. As you move past addiction and begin creating this new vision of the person you want to become, you'll find that there's beauty and perspective in having that past experience in your rearview mirror. That's called wisdom.

POSITIVE REBELLION

Addiction, in my belief, is about being fixated on what we think we are. This often means not wanting to walk the straight-arrow path and conform with societal norms. Because we are so hungry to rebel against anything that feels associated with the white-picket-fence lifestyle, we decide to do the exact opposite, and we do it to such a degree that we rebel ourselves right into a fucked-up and reckless state of being.

I made the same mistake myself. Now that all this time has passed and I can look back on it with a more objective point of view, I've realized something interesting. Our instinct to go against the grain isn't a weakness; it's actually one of our greatest strengths. We just haven't been using it the right way.

People make the mistake of thinking they're not strong enough to create their reality on their own. And unfortunately, there don't seem to be many options presented to us other than those boring life clichés.

"Get good grades."

"Get into a good college."

"Get married."

"Buy a house."

"Have children."

"Save for retirement."

As most of us understood from a young age, all these clichés really add up to the same thing: "Live a boring life inside the box and die a restless death without ever questioning if you lived the life you really wanted."

If your goal is to have a traditional 9-to-5 and feel good about having some structure in your life, that's perfectly fine. But the thing is, some of us don't actually want to spend our lives living in Pleasantville, USA. Not everyone has the same wants. We all have our own hopes and dreams, most of which don't conform to the boring and pointless ideals that society lays out for us.

It's no wonder that people who call themselves and their peers "lifelong addicts" can't seem to ever get their shit together. Even into their fifties, people believe there is still something cool and rebellious in being an addict. It makes them seem like a partier, someone who has lived a colorful life. The cool cat. The mysterious girl you can't seem to figure out. The dope dude who just can't be wrangled in. But if you know better, you quickly realize that this is someone who is still aching to be the younger, cooler version of themselves that they used to be. They keep one foot in adolescence at all times. In doing so, they keep a part of themselves stuck in the cycle of addiction as well. It's funny. Not only does this way of thinking hold people back from overcoming addiction, but it also makes them feel like they need to suppress that contrarian, rebellious energy they feel in their heart.

It makes them feel like they need to extinguish the best parts of themselves.

Seriously, take a second to think about it. Many addicts and former addicts share this quality. This restless spirit of rebellion. Instead of applying this energy to something useful, many of us have made the mistake of drowning it through substance addiction. So what if, in the process of overcoming addiction, putting the old self in the rearview, and creating the new self, we figured out how to channel that rebellious spirit for something... amazing?

Imagine that if instead of rebelling through addiction, we rebelled in a way that was productive to ourselves and to the versions of our future selves we are trying to create? If addiction is about focusing on our current actions and the person we've become, what if we could shift to getting hooked on forming new habits and a fresh identity? What if in the spirit of rebellion against the "white picket fence" lifestyle, we created an alternative mindset that gave us that same thrill of going against the grain for something that was, in fact, positive?

This is a core part of what you can take as the seeds for the new self you are going to create. So instead of constantly looking backward, you will be full steam ahead on the new life you're going to build.

But I want you to remember something.

This is important.

Just because you have addiction in your past *does not mean* you need to throw away every part of yourself that was present or contributed to who you used to be. You are not an addict because of your best qualities, whether those qualities are rebelliousness or fearlessness or being the smartest person in the room. Don't worry; you can still be cool. You became an addict because you became addicted to using substances to mask the parts of yourself you didn't like and to run away from things in your past, present, or future that you were too afraid to face.

Once you face these things, you can finally let go of the old self and permanently leave it in the past. You can find gratitude for the fact that you still have time to turn your life around—and embrace your best qualities to pursue whatever you want next.

CHAPTER 10

DEPENDENCY VS. HEALTHY RELATIONSHIPS

According to the Five Chimps theory, you can predict the mood and behavior of one chimp by observing the five chimps they hang out with most. The same is true for you and me.

If our core relationships are built on a foundation of dependency, we're headed for a massive lack of accountability and all the suffering that comes along with it. Think about the kind of people you meet in Anonymous meetings. On what basis are these relationships formed? Are meetings designed to promote relationships with healthy boundaries? Or do they create friendships that are entirely dependent on people subscribing to a common ideology, being discouraged from thinking about addiction on their own terms, and following a strict set of rules?

Psh. Talk about the blind leading the blind.

DISCONNECTING FROM DEPENDENCY AND TOXICITY

Disconnecting from the negative things in your life will give you the space you need to change. Yes, it can suck sometimes. I'm sure some of your addict friends are great to be around. But unless you want to be an addict for the rest of your life, I suggest you take a step back.

Some people will argue with me and say, "But AA is my community." But what they're really saying is "I'd rather sit around telling stories with other addicts then actually do the hard, raunchy work that is required." The question at the center of it remains the same: do you want to tell yourself you're changing, or do you actually want to change?

Disconnecting completely from others means letting go of the people you were associated with—buying from, drinking with, using with, etc. Most likely this means disconnecting from these people completely. Other types of relationships may only need to be disconnected temporarily, such as family, spouses, exes you share children with, or close friends. Sometimes, limiting these interactions and allowing yourself not to get distracted will help you redirect your focus back to your new self.

But it doesn't stop there. As you move forward and leave unhealthy relationships behind, you have to start shifting your focus to people and relationships that are aligned with the person you want to become.

ROMANTIC PARTNERS

Quick story time. During a time in my life when I went through a hard breakup, I had to constantly remind myself of a lesson I learned earlier in my life: the energy flows where the attention goes. I'll be honest. For a second I was stuck after my relationship ended. I did the same things we all do: I avoided taking responsibility. I vented. I let myself cope instead of overcoming my emotions, and I was full of excuses that were keeping me clinging to the past. But once I finally removed my ex from my life, I started to move on. Instead of my attention being stuck on my ex, my attention returned to myself, and I began seeing the reality of my relationship.

I started analyzing myself and thinking about what I had been putting up with. Why I had attracted this experience. I started diving into *my own* behaviors because, after all, I had no control over my partner's actions. I had to build the self control to walk away. It's not what I wanted at the time, but I knew I had to get to work on creating a new vision for myself that focused on what I wanted to find in my next romantic relationship.

Now it's your turn. Take a hard look at your romantic relationships. Are they pushing you toward the new self you want to actualize? Or are they holding you back? Just like you should be creating a vision for the life that you want, you should be including what type of partner you see yourself having in that vision as well. How do they make you feel? Do they frustrate or inspire you? Suffocate or support you? And maybe most importantly, what does their vision look like? Because if you're with someone who doesn't have a vision for themselves, then I'm afraid they are probably not a person who is going to have any respect for yours.

BEST FRIENDS

The person you call your "best friend" shouldn't be the same person who is costing you your health. Whether you do it today, tomorrow, or seven years from now, you're not going to be able to make any real changes if your go-to person is contributing to your bad behavior. You have to ask yourself who is and who is not serving you. As hard as it can be to let go, you have to take care of yourself before you can begin to be selfless.

But I know this isn't easy—just take it from me.

At the age of twenty-four, I had two best friends.

FRAGMENT—MAY AND TIM

Tim's been my best friend for the last eight years. Our friendship has been through a lot. There was a period when Tim and I were drug addicts and partied together. We lived together off and on during these times.

When we lived together most recently, we were both sober. Well, at least at first.

Living with Tim again was going great until he started bringing some questionable new friends around. He told me not to worry about them and promised he'd been staying clean. But after what I had been through, I knew bullshit when I saw it, and I wasn't going to be a witness to it. So I went to live with a mutual friend. This was a few months ago.

He's been reaching out excessively, wanting me back in his life. I normally give him my usual response: "I don't want to be around you if you're high."

He had given me an old laptop, and now he's saying he needs it back. I know this is just out of shame and he's using the laptop as an excuse to try to reconnect, but I give in and decide to meet him in his parking lot.

I get there, and Tim doesn't come down. I already know the reason he's late—classic meth addict move. I wait around for about half an hour before I decide to leave.

Two days go by, and I don't hear from Tim.

My phone is ringing. It's Kelsey.

"Hey what's up?" I say.

She responds in a casual tone. "Hey, did you hear that Tim died? Took his dog for a walk and overdosed on the sidewalk."

I fall to the floor.

FRAGMENT—APRIL AND MAY

It's been a year since I got the call about Tim.

I'm sitting on the couch with my girlfriend watching TV. We just started dating recently, and I'm excited for her and April to meet.

My phone buzzes. It's a text from a mutual friend of ours.

"What happened to April?"

What does she mean, "What happened to April?" I just talked to her two days ago.

I drop my phone and run to my car. I start driving toward April's house. I'm going to go find April, I think.

I get to her house, but she's not there.

I storm in to find April's dad and sister crying on the couch.

Here's the backstory:

I lived with April and her mom for a short period of time during high school.

April's mother was an alcoholic. Until one day April walked into the bathroom and found her dead on the toilet.

April became an alcoholic not too long after that. She was drinking so excessively that she was downing an entire bottle of vodka every day.

A few weeks after her mom died, her cat got run over by a car.

A few months after that, I was putting on makeup in my bathroom one night, and I got a call. My phone was in the other room, so I didn't answer and kept getting ready. Then the phone rang again. *Oh shit,* I thought. I ran to my phone and saw it was April. I knew something was wrong because she and I had an agreement that if one of us called twice, it meant something bad had happened.

I answered the phone, and April sounded distraught. She was crying uncontrollably. It was hard to make out what she was saying. I told her to take deep breaths so I could understand what was going on. She told me that she had been walking home from a bar, and a homeless man had come from around the corner, grabbed her, thrown her into the dirt, and raped her.

I was completely shattered.

After this series of tragic events, there was a period where she was doing better. April got a great job, and she wasn't drinking. Things were starting to look up for her.

Come to find out on the night she died, April had decided to go out with some friends from work. She ended up "relapsing" and using alcohol and cocaine. When she got home, she told her sister that her heart was hurting.

"Do you want me to take you to the hospital?" her sister asked.

"No. I just want to lie down," April said.

When April's sister went into April's bedroom the next morning, she found her twenty-seven-year-old sister splayed over the edge of the bed, her lifeless body purple from head to toe.

People use the term "best friend" so loosely. It's not me saying, "One of my best friends died." *These were my two best friends.*

The reason I share these stories is not so you'll feel bad for me but so you will let go of the "what if" mentality and accept that fate is out of our hands and that we are all responsible for ourselves.

FAMILY

As you know by now, your environment and the people in it play a key role in your well-being. But that doesn't mean you have to prioritize your relationships the same way other people do. People like to say things like "Family comes first." But if your parents abuse you, then your family should absolutely *not* come first. Longtime friends will often say, "Friends till the end!" But if your closest friendships are with a bunch of addicts who are constantly bringing you down, then you have to understand there's nothing healthy about prioritizing these friendships.

HEALTHY RELATIONSHIPS

It's a core part of our human nature to strive for deep, meaningful, and healthy connections with other people.

Why would we settle for anything less?

When people are doing drugs, they magnetize other addicts. Have you noticed that? We all huddle up in these groups we make, kinda like biker gangs, *Sex and the City* girls, hippies, festival goers, video gamers, or Dungeons and Dragons nerds. Whatever you spend your time doing, chances are you'll end up magnetizing other people who care about the same things. So the big question you have to ask yourself is this: what are you magnetizing?

Once you've accomplished this goal of freeing yourself from negative relationships and you're no longer dependent on relationships that are contributing to your negative actions, you will be able to transform from your old self to your new self. You will be able to move into any situation, even if it involves a person from the past who used to draw you into bad behavior. Once you've transformed, you will be different. The conversations will be different. Your behaviors will be different. Your feelings will be different. Therefore, your reality will be different.

Healthy relationships create healthy outcomes. They inspire us. They make us feel held, supported, and connected. Having people around you who are happy, healthy, and successful brings a positive energy to your life that you really can't get anywhere else.

They add more value to your life than you would have ever imagined possible.

CHAPTER 11

TEMPTATION VS. MOTIVATION

"What you resist persists."

—CARL JUNG

TEMPTATION

Isn't it funny how treating your addiction like a temptation makes it so much harder to overcome? It turns something objectively toxic and destructive into something that feels desirable. Should resisting temptation really be the basis of your approach to beating addiction? This is like telling people to hold off on eating that delicious brownie because of the excess sugar. Because you know what? A brownie sounds really nice every once in a while.

In reality, this is completely misguided. I mean, come on. As you and I both know, the thing you're addicted to is no brownie. It's a toxic chemical or compound that gives you momentary pleasure in exchange for all-but-certain destruction to your relationships, career, and life. What's so tempting about that? If drugs were actually pleasurable in any real sense, you wouldn't be reading a book about how to overcome your shitty addiction. Having to ingest something on a daily basis in order to feel good isn't sustainable. Because you're not actually becoming more of who you are—you're just continuing to be the person you no longer want to be.

Unless you have a sugar or food addiction, you can safely eat a brownie here and there without it making a crazy impact. But for drug addicts, we all know that one little taste will turn into an "every weekend" thing and eventually become a core part of our everyday experience. I know this firsthand because it's exactly what happened to me. I even wrote about it in my journal during my school days.

Can't wait to get out of school so we can do IT again.

That's why this idea of temptation needs to be reframed. Instead of looking at drugs or alcohol as a temptation, which is a form of still living in the past, we can look forward to things that motivate and inspire us to be who we really want to be. I might sound like a broken record at this point, but getting you to understand this point is essential. Looking at substances as something you have to abstain from—as this amazing thing you and everyone you know really wants to do—makes drugs and alcohol seem appealing in a dark and mysterious kind of way. Like a can of Bud Light is that apple on the tree and you're Adam and Eve, willing to risk it all for just a little taste.

You have to remove the very notion of addiction being a temptation. And unless your definition of being motivated is "taking it one day at a time," then we have some work to do.

NON-ADDICTS AND TEMPTATION

It's important that we take a moment to talk about non-addicts too. In the 12-step world, people are often discouraged from being around others who use drugs and alcohol in a more recreational fashion. Here's the truth: there is absolutely nothing wrong with people who occasionally drink a glass of wine or smoke a joint once in a while. Hell, there's nothing wrong with someone enjoying a little mushroom trip in the middle of Joshua Tree for a psychedelic healing sesh.

Let's be clear: the line between recreational user and closeted addict can be thin. If those same people I described above are counting down the days until they can take their next drink or hit, then it's clear that they are on the verge of having a problem. But we have to understand that there are plenty of people out there who can use drugs and alcohol in a way that is not detrimental to their health or quality of life. To paint the picture, take my dad for instance: every Friday he loves cracking open a bottle of wine and pouring himself a glass or two. But does he think about drinking wine at work all week or obsess over it? No. He loves hiking with his buddies and swimming at the gym every day, and when the weekend comes, he enjoys his glass of wine. There is no addiction. And he's certainly not running away from his reality.

Once we accept this as a possibility, the question becomes this: how do we decide how to approach these things ourselves? By no means am I saying you should keep lying to yourself and telling yourself that you aren't actually an addict and you can have a drink every now and then. Sorry, dude. I'm talking about whether future you—your new self who has overcome your addiction completely—can ever become a social drinker or a recreational user.

The truth is that no one can answer these questions but you. No one is going to be keeping tabs on you either (unless you're in rehab, have a sober companion, or are still living under your parents' roof). Let's say one day in the future you decide you have become fully awakened and you have addressed all your ticks and triggers. So you go to a music festival and someone hands you Molly. What do you do? We know what your NA group and your sponsor would say. They would tell you that you don't have the right to make that decision for yourself. That the answer is an absolute no. But how do you really feel? Because in truth, if you have actually moved on and no longer have interest in going back to your old self, you might agree with your instinct that you can safely have an occasional drink or every-once-in-a-while party drug if you want. Because clearly, spontaneously taking Molly and jamming out to some music isn't the same thing as snorting coke every day.

GATEWAY DRUGS

Then there's the argument people make about "gateway drugs." Psh. What a pathetic excuse!

When you have an experience with drugs or drinking, you are either going to hate it or love it. No one can say, "Oooo...but, hey, Amanda, if you're gonna try ketamine, that means you're gonna be addicted to heroin tomorrow." Wrong! You, in your nature, are the only person who is going to know what you will truly gravitate to and what you could potentially become addicted to. Like I said in the beginning, if you are gravitating toward substance abuse, it's because you're escaping something. So no, I wouldn't blame "gateway drugs" for turning you into an addict. If I were you, I'd blame myself. Grasping the concept yet?

Whether or not you can consume drugs or alcohol causally is a complicated issue that you should take seriously. Really listen to yourself. No one is holding you accountable here. If you truly want to move on, you are the only person who can do it. If you're lying to yourself, you're only cheating yourself. Unlike AA, there is no chip system here. There is *you,* and there are *your lies.* That's it.

Remember, if you can truly say to yourself—without the lie detector going off—"I've moved on. I am no longer that person, so I can have a glass of wine when I'm out at dinner tonight. This isn't something that can ever spiral me back into my old self because my new self is nothing like that," then great! Record yourself saying it, and then watch it back to see if you believe the person talking. Because if so, and if you really have moved on, then don't feel like you have to continue being limited by the mistakes of your past. If your new self is someone who lives a disciplined life and occasionally wants to have a drink, I'm the last person who's going to tell you to doubt yourself. I'm just the person suggesting that you start asking the questions!

This is great because people lie all the time. Do you know how I know this? From the experience of being lied to and from doing the lying myself! Currently, there are eight billion people on this planet, which means there are millions of different scenarios for all of us. All I'm asking is are you a liar? And to whom? Yourself? Who's really listening? And why do you care?

Life is not meant to be lived in constant restraint or suffocation. Life, triggers, and desires look so very different to all of us.

Say, for example, I was to introduce you to Daphne. Daphne used to be a big-time drinker. *Big time.* Like a three-bottles-of-white-wine-a-night kind of gal. The kind who would sit there in her atrium chatting it up on the phone for hours, getting all riled up with her girlfriends, chain smoking Marlboro Lights, and talking smack about her boyfriend. There came a point where Daphne woke up to the real reason she drank so much. She was able to realize that the trauma stemmed from her dad leaving her when she was young. She never forgave him and ended up taking it out on her boyfriend, but only when she felt confident to do so. That was where the intoxication came in. That was fifteen years ago.

Today Daphne is married with a kid. She and her husband own a winery up in Napa, California. She occasionally has a glass of wine or participates in a tasting. Does she still carry around the ghost of her father, her experience as an alcoholic, and the rest of her past mistakes? No. But she's not going to try to convince you of it. She only values her own opinion of herself and knows what she's found to be true.

Let's shine a light on substance abuse and call it out for what it really is. It's short-term reward for long-term damage. It's sacrificing your future for some empty pleasure in the moment. When we view addiction in this way, we can trade out that mystique that comes with temptation for something that is much more valuable: motivation.

MOTIVATION

If you want to stay motivated, remind yourself of your vision. It may seem repetitive, but trust me: there's nothing more sobering (pun intended) than looking at a journal entry or whiteboard that lists out the vision you've established for your new self. **Because what you focus on grows, and what you ignore dies.**

You can think about it as taking advice from one of two people: your old self, who is a reckless drug addict, or your new self, the boss motherfucker who gets what they want out of life. Which version of yourself would you like to be?

Another good way to stay motivated is to change your frame of mind from telling yourself, "I have to do this" or "I need to do that," to "I get to do this" and "I am blessed that I have the opportunity to do that." This shift might seem subtle, but boy is it powerful. I wake up every day genuinely grateful that I get to take care of myself and give my mind, body, and spirit the things they need in order to thrive. I can't wait to take on the day. With your temptation tissues safely in the trashcan and newly found motivation in hand, it's time that you start waking up and doing the same.

Earlier I listed out all the things that described my life when I was a meth addict jonesing for my next hit. Nowadays, I'm getting everything I want out of life with a nice big *fuck you* mentality for anyone who thinks I could have gotten here any other way. Here's a glimpse into what my life looks like today:

- I'm the founder and CEO of an IT company.
- I have a beautiful home in Los Angeles, California.

- I own the cars and toys I never thought I would be able to afford.
- I have a healthy and active lifestyle.
- I have my daily spiritual practice.
- I travel to new places and experience new and vibrant cultures.
- I have successful and inspiring friends.
- I have a loving and supportive family.
- I get the opportunity to show people struggling with addiction what life is like outside of the never-ending recovery cycle and what it truly means to overcome it.

Like I've been saying, I'm not telling you these details about my life so you can go and try to copy and paste them onto your own. Just like how my struggle may have been different from yours, your goals may be different than mine. I wanted to include these details about my life so you can understand that a radical transformation from *drug addict* to *100 percent renewed being* is truly possible.

If someone who knew me in the past were to see my life now, I don't think they'd believe they were looking at the same person.

When the people who know you now see you five or ten years down the road, who are they going to see?

ANONYMOUS REIMAGINED

I, too, have a vision for addicts who are looking for a way out. But unlike Bill and Bob, I'm not going to create some cookie-cutter mold and try to stuff everyone into it. As it relates to Anonymous groups, I've always questioned what they see as the bigger picture. Instead of making these institutions a haven for bitching and moaning, we could create environments that foster radical change that inspires people to move past their addict selves and on to something better. Is there a way to improve these organizations so that they become less fear-driven and more action-focused? Like, what if we updated these programs and turned AA houses into motivational speaker workshops? Traded unqualified sponsors out for certified coaches and therapists? What might the state of addiction recovery look like then?

As nice as this sounds, I'm not sure if we'll ever get there. People hate change, and when an organization has been around for so long, most people just stop questioning it.

This is why we must return to the only real solution that exists in front of us: doing the work ourselves.

CHAPTER 12

THE NEW SELF

A WARRIOR MINDSET

In AA, they tell you to live in a state of constantly rehashing the past—which, without you realizing it, has been creating your present.

I'm here to tell you there's a better way. A brighter, lighter, and more optimistic way that doesn't feel forced but instead allows you to guide yourself to a life beyond suffering.

We were not put on this earth to suffer. We were put here to enjoy life, love each other, and create one-of-a-kind lives for ourselves that are full of everything we want. I know this might sound like a load of bullshit that you hear all the time, but it really is true. Sure, you could spend your time going to meetings and living in the past, telling yourself that you've fucked it all up and it's too late to make anything of yourself. And everyone in those meetings will be nodding their heads, saying, "Me too, brother."

But you could also say fuck that.

You could instead work through the demons of your past and then leave it all behind. For you and everyone else reading this book, there is the possibility of an amazing future out there. So why the rush to hurry up and wait? Sure, most people diddle-daddle around their lives, suppressing every emotion, not able to make a change or break their habits in time to experience the magic that exists on the other side of the unknown. But then again, you're not most people. In fact, you're completely unique. There's no one else like you. Did you know that there isn't another human on this planet with the same fingerprint?

I lived in hiding for a very long time as an addict. When I get asked today why I don't drink or "party" and how even after I overcame my addiction I could stay up all night partying without needing anything, I simply say that addiction is in my past. It was nothing more than an experience, and I have zero interest in ever going back. I see the confusion in their eyes. I see that I've made them uncomfortable. I see how unbelievable they think it is for me to be so unbothered by it all. This is because I've triggered these individuals, which makes them automatically judge themselves and become resentful of their jealousy toward me. My life now is not the same as it was before. I don't sit here and think about it every day; that memory doesn't ever come up anymore, unlike the addicts who go to the daily or weekly meetings to constantly remind themselves of their old selves and keep that negative energy in motion.

To say that I'm repulsed by the thought of returning to the person I was is an understatement.

I truly have no desire to go back to living in a false reality. I love myself too much, and once I realized this simple truth, I've never been tempted to go back. Many people have this idea that they have to make every day an "honest day," which, in this sense, means to talk about and relive their addiction in order to avoid slipping back into it. In reality, those people haven't moved on. Once you move on from your past and truly become new, you no longer have any interest in returning to your old self. If a man comes out of the closet and tells the world he's gay, does he feel the need to attend meetings to make sure he doesn't slip back into the life of passing as a straight man? No. He's finally accepted himself for who he really is, and as a result, he can be his truest self without giving a damn about what anyone else thinks about it.

As our time together comes to a close, let me remind you one last time that we all have our own opinions. None of us are cut from the same cloth. We all have different upbringings, different traumas, different causes for our addiction.

Like I've said throughout this book, only you can tap into what those causes are and uncover what the solutions look like. No one can ever overcome your addiction for you. No one can grab you by the hand and drag you out of addiction and into a new and better life. You have to do it on your own. **You get to do it on your own.**

Do your own work. Find your own answers. Become the new you.

There might have been an old part of you that picked up this book looking for the easy way out. That weak part of yourself that wanted to take the blue pill instead of the red pill. But even in *The Matrix*, Neo had to face himself to see the truth. He had to accept the fact that the only real choice is to no longer live in denial. He learned that he had to experience a brutal rebirth in order to benefit from the freedom that came only with recognizing the false reality he had been living in. Once you are awakened, you will never want to go back to living a lie.

Remember that the road to self-discovery is never-ending. For your entire life, you will always be exploring and learning more about yourself. Discovering the root of your addiction, however, is a journey that does have an end.

Moving from the old to the new will have its challenging moments. Shoot, it might get so uncomfortable that you want to reject the feeling and run away from it. This is your brain sending your body a signal that you're in unfamiliar territory. The trick is to become familiar with the unfamiliar until it becomes your new normal.

After a couple of weeks of fighting with yourself, you'll start to realize that your old thoughts are no longer a desire. When that same trigger arises in the future, you'll think back to the mentality you had when you were an addict, and your brain will automatically say, "Nah—switch!" Your mind will turn to your new thoughts and focus on your new desires. This process is often unconscious and is the true result of rewiring. Because these negative thoughts from the past don't match your new vision. They've lost their emotional charge, and therefore the feeling is gone. You've beaten it. Just don't get cocky. Continue to fight for yourself until truth rings the doorbell and you finally answer the door.

My parting words to you: embrace the ups and downs. Embrace the discomfort. Embrace the disapproval from anyone who tries to tell you that you are sick, that you are destined to be an addict for the rest of your life. Because you know what? It's all a part of the journey.

Learn to let go more quickly. Give yourself permission to truly soar. Keep your sights set on your future, regardless of what your current circumstances or hardships might look like. Remember that the road is smoother up ahead.

Set your own goals. Just like how you shouldn't try to copy and paste some bullshit 12-step program into your life, don't copy and paste the things in this book either. Take the bits and pieces that you've connected with, and apply them every day moving forward.

And then move on. If you read this book to the end, there's a really good chance that your old self is under the spotlight, and you're ready to move on. Keep moving forward toward self-discovery, self-actualization, and self-mastery. Once you can attain happiness within yourself and conquer your addiction, leave it all behind. This is the truest testament to having overcome your addiction. Not some group. Not some steps. Not a life sentence to recovery.

This is freedom. This is your future. And this is your life.

I would wish you luck on your journey, but since you have learned that you don't need luck—or anything else outside of yourself, for that matter—I guess I'll just leave you with this piece of advice: next time someone asks you how long you've been sober, smile at them and say:

Please, don't call me sober.

Call me _____.

OPTIONS FOR TREATMENT AND ASSISTANCE

TREATMENT

DETOX

Detoxification is the process of removing toxins from your bloodstream. There are certain drugs that require medically assisted detox, including opioids (such as OxyContin, Percocet, Vicodin, fentanyl, morphine, codeine, heroin, etc.) and alcohol when the severity of the dependency is great enough that sudden stoppage could result in death.

If you are unsure of whether you need to detox, please go see a medical professional and do this the right way. As I said earlier in the book, even the best plan for overcoming addiction only works if you are alive to see it through. If a detox is what you need at this moment, I feel for you. Hang in there. Be responsible, and do what is best for your long-term health.

REHAB

Going to rehab is like taking a vacation and then getting back home and realizing, "Oh right, nothing's changed...have I?"

More than 80 percent of my clients have all said the same thing, that rehab was nothing like real life. So why do it?

If your intentions are good, then rehab can serve as a reset. A way to disconnect from your environment and your current circumstances so you can become aware of what you're doing to yourself. So you can work on it and reframe it. But if you're not actually thinking about the root cause of your issues, then rehab offers you little more than a very expensive break from reality.

However much progress you make, you will still have to return to the real world and take responsibility for your actions moving forward. There will be no glorified babysitter coming home with you. Well, unless you hire a hand-holding sober companion...

I'm sorry, but just because you've been to rehab doesn't mean you've done any of the work required to change. When you walk into a rehab center, you'll likely find a bunch of people lounging around watching movies, reading books, and going to meetings two or three times a day until their thirty, sixty, or ninety days are up. Talk about a pricey way to accomplish nothing.

They also have what are called "life skills." You can walk from room to room and find everything from art and cooking classes to podcasting recording studios and 3D printing labs. What these "life skills" are trying to do is to give you a task. And what are these tasks doing, exactly? Distracting you.

Are you taking these life skills out of rehab with you? Unless you are going to become a professional podcaster or a 3D printing technician, these "skills" you're learning in rehab are probably not applicable to your real life.

When you go to rehab, you're pressing pause on your life. And then when you come back home, you press play and find yourself in the exact same position as before.

And you know what's funny? I've even had clients tell me that they extended their insurance just so they could stay longer. Umm...suppression much? So what you're telling me is you're scared to go back to the real world? Well, guess what, honey? You can't live at rehab forever...or can you? Many people treat rehab just like AA—they hold out for as long as they can, and if they "relapse," they know they can always go back.

With a rehab center, we all know how expensive that shit is. Which is why it *can* be effective in the right situations—because it requires a person to take action and get themselves to a place where they can take over their recovery journey on their own. So if you need to go to rehab, get in there and do the work. Then get the hell out before the bank account hits zero.

ASSISTANCE
INTERVENTIONS

This is a coin toss. And quite frankly, I'm not a fan of leaving a person's future up to chance.

Again, everyone's process is different. While I do like the idea of a wake-up call, people have to come to their own realizations about their addiction. When you put a bunch of people in a room and have them more or less shaming a friend or loved one, the intervention becomes more about the expectations of the people involved and less about the individual's personal journey to overcoming their addiction. This means that during their journey, instead of having the support of friends and family, those same individuals create a feeling of pressure that can add weight to the person who is trying to make a change. It also interrupts the focus they're trying to place on themselves.

Shame in general doesn't work for everyone. For instance, sometimes a person is shamed into looking at themselves and feeling so embarrassed about what they're doing that they actually do change. For someone else, this could lead them to retreat deeper into their shame and make them even more avoidant. While, of course, there are stories of people for whom an intervention has worked, the reality is that if you want to make a change, it's unrealistic to expect your loved ones to throw you another intervention every time you decide to stay the same.

THERAPY

Therapy can be a fantastic resource when used the right way. It can also be a waste of time if you approach it with the wrong intentions.

A lifelong therapist will let you rant about your feelings like an Anonymous group without interruption. Just like the group, they will often give you coping mechanisms to help you deal with the immediate challenges you are facing. The problem that often arises with therapy is that some therapists and patients treat therapy like a lifelong coping mechanism—one with no end date in sight—to complain about how they just can't seem to manage life on their own. Aw. Poor you.

When I go into therapy, I know that it's temporary. I would never see a therapist on an ongoing basis. I choose to go to a therapist when I recognize that I have some issues that I need professional help with working my way through—not because I need someone to hold my hand through the various ups and downs of everyday life. I'm also very particular about what I look for in a therapist. I always seek out one who will be able to offer me solutions for overcoming myself rather than short-term methods for coping. And if a therapist I'm considering is unaware of the difference, then that makes my considerations that much easier. Therapists are human too, so I'm not talking down on therapists as a whole, but just like with any other profession, there are bad therapists, mediocre therapists, good therapists, and exceptional therapists.

At the end of the day, you know what's best for you. If you are participating in a therapy session and you realize you're just using your therapist as someone who will listen to you bitch and moan, then you have to take responsibility for the situation and accept that you aren't making any progress. During a difficult breakup, I sought out a therapist to help me through my failed relationship and saw that she was only enabling me and my bullshit. So I dropped her like a hot potato and enrolled myself with another therapist. Sure enough, the four weeks I spent with that therapist hit me like a slap in the face and gave me the wake-up call I desperately needed to check myself. I also ended up realizing that the process of overcoming my breakup followed the exact same path as overcoming my addiction, and I had to redirect the energy I was pushing outward onto myself.

This goes to show that growth is a lifelong journey and that the skills you learn through overcoming your addiction will apply to obstacles you'll face throughout the rest of your life.

My advice is that if you're looking for a therapist, find one who can provide the same level of insight for you.

PLANT MEDICINE

Some people think that plant medicine and drugs are the same. They aren't. A drug is something you are abusing and chemically dependent on—something you're using to escape yourself. Plant medicine facilitates a temporary experience that could offer you a deeper look into yourself.

It's important that I say you don't *need* plant medicine. If you are interested in using the experiences provided by supervised psychedelic healing sessions or shaman-guided retreats to go deeper into yourself, then plants can be a great resource.

From my own experience, I can say that plant medicine, rituals, reiki healings, meditation, and breathwork have allowed me to have euphoric, mystical experiences that have shown me unrealized parts of myself. There are a lot of people who preach that plant medicine is a key to overcoming your addiction—and while it can definitely be useful, it's not for everyone. Do your own research, and decide whether it's right for you.

ACKNOWLEDGMENTS

Thank you to those who inspired me to publish by confirming the necessity of this book.

Thank you to you, the reader, for keeping an open mind and for the opportunity to share this book with you. Especially those of you who feel the same way.

Thank you to my clients who were willing to be vulnerable and open up to me, and for trusting me with the most intimate details of your lives.

Thank you to my family for putting up with all the shitty things I did. Thank you for forgiving me and, most of all, for *forgetting* who I used to be. And for *moving on* with me.

Thank you to April and Tim for the hard lessons. And among it all, for being my friends.

And lastly, I want to thank myself for having the courage to be a dick and stand up to this worldwide organization and call out its flaws. As I say in the book: "For better or for worse, I'm charging forward with a smile on my face and zero fucks to give about what anyone else has to say about it."

MAY'S RECOMMENDED READINGS AND TEACHINGS

BOOKS

- *Breaking the Habit of Being Yourself* by Joe Dispenza
- *The School of Greatness* by Lewis Howes
- *Personal Power* by Tony Robbins
- *12 Rules for Life: An Antidote to Chaos* by Jordan Peterson
- *Awareness* by Anthony de Mello
- *Be Here Now* by Ram Dass
- *Spirit Junkie* by Gabby Bernstein

SPEECHES, YOUTUBE CHANNELS, AND DOCUMENTARIES

- *Impact Theory* with Tom Bilyeu (YouTube)
- *Becoming Nobody* by Ram Dass (documentary)
- *The Call to Courage* by Brené Brown (documentary)
- *The Power of Vulnerability* by Brené Brown (TED Talk)
- Audible programs by Esther and Abraham Hicks
- *Progressive* by Joe Dispenza (course)
- *Rewired with Dr. Joe Dispenza* (television series)

www.ingramcontent.com/pod-product-compliance
Lightning Source LLC
Chambersburg PA
CBHW060525080526
44586CB00012B/616